Approaches to learning and teaching

Literature in English

a toolkit for international teachers

Peter Thomas

Series Editors: Paul Ellis and Lauren Harris

CAMBRIDGE
UNIVERSITY PRESS

Shaftesbury Road, Cambridge CB2 8EA, United Kingdom

One Liberty Plaza, 20th Floor, New York, NY 10006, USA

477 Williamstown Road, Port Melbourne, VIC 3207, Australia

314–321, 3rd Floor, Plot 3, Splendor Forum, Jasola District Centre, New Delhi – 110025, India

103 Penang Road, #05–06/07, Visioncrest Commercial, Singapore 238467

Cambridge University Press is part of the University of Cambridge.

It furthers the University's mission by disseminating knowledge in the pursuit of education, learning and research at the highest international levels of excellence.

www.cambridge.org
Information on this title: www.cambridge.org/9781316645895 (Paperback)

© Cambridge Assessment International Education 2018

® IGCSE is a registered trademark

First published 2018

20 19 18 17 16 15 14 13 12 11 10 9 8 7

Printed in Great Britain by Ashford Colour Press Ltd.

A catalogue record for this publication is available from the British Library

ISBN 978-1-316-64589-5 Paperback

Contents

Online lesson ideas and a glossary for this book can be found at cambridge.org/9781316645895

Acknowledgements

The authors and publishers acknowledge the following sources of copyright material and are grateful for the permissions granted. While every effort has been made, it has not always been possible to identify the sources of all the material used, or to trace all copyright holders. If any omissions are brought to our notice, we will be happy to include the appropriate acknowledgements on reprinting.

Chapter 9 extract from 'Nothing's Changed' by Tatamkhulu Afrika, used by permission of NB Publishers; Chapter 9 extract from 'Checking out Me History' by John Agard, used by permission of Bloodaxe Books; Chapter 11 extract from 'Presents from My Aunts in Pakistan' by Moniza Alvi, used by permission of Bloodaxe Books

Lesson Ideas 3.4 and 6.3 extract from *An Inspector Calls* by J.B. Priestley, published and used with permission by Penguin Random House, and United Agents; Lesson Idea 5.1 'Nettles' by Vernon Scannell, used by permission of the Author's Estate; Lesson Idea 5.2 extract from *Mr Pip* by Lloyd Jones, published and used by permission of Penguin Random House Inc, and Penguin Random House Canada, and The Text Publishing Company; Lesson Idea 9.6 'Portrait of a Machine' by Louis Untermeyer. Illustration by and used by kind permission of Laurie Rudling.

Thanks to the following for permission to reproduce images:
Cover image bgblue/Getty Images
Inside in order of appearance HeyHeyDesigns/Getty Images; Cultura RM Exclusive/PhotoStock-Israel/Getty Images; Photo by Fine Art Images/Heritage Images/Getty Images

Introduction to the series by the editors

1

1 Approaches to learning and teaching Literature in English

This series of books is the result of close collaboration between Cambridge University Press and Cambridge Assessment International Education, both departments of the University of Cambridge. The books are intended as a companion guide for teachers, to supplement your learning and provide you with extra resources for the lessons you are planning. Their focus is deliberately not syllabus-specific, although occasional reference has been made to programmes and qualifications. We want to invite you to set aside for a while assessment objectives and grading, and take the opportunity instead to look in more depth at how you teach your subject and how you motivate and engage with your students.

The themes presented in these books are informed by evidence-based research into what works to improve students' learning and pedagogical best practices. To ensure that these books are first and foremost practical resources, we have chosen not to include too many academic references, but we have provided some suggestions for further reading.

We have further enhanced the books by asking the authors to create accompanying lesson ideas. These are described in the text and can be found in a dedicated space online. We hope the books will become a dynamic and valid representation of what is happening now in learning and teaching in the context in which you work.

Our organisations also offer a wide range of professional development opportunities for teachers. These range from syllabus- and topic-specific workshops and large-scale conferences to suites of accredited qualifications for teachers and school leaders. Our aim is to provide you with valuable support, to build communities and networks, and to help you both enrich your own teaching methodology and evaluate its impact on your students.

Each of the books in this series follows a similar structure. In the third chapter, we have asked our authors to consider the essential elements of their subject, the main concepts that might be covered in a school curriculum, and why these are important. The next chapters give you a brief guide on how to interpret a syllabus or subject guide, and how to plan a programme of study. The authors will encourage you to think too about what is not contained in a syllabus and how you can pass on your own passion for the subject you teach.

The main body of the text takes you through those aspects of learning and teaching which are widely recognised as important. We would like to stress that there is no single recipe for excellent teaching, and that different schools, operating in different countries and cultures, will have strong traditions that should be respected. There is a growing consensus, however, about some important practices and approaches that need to be adopted if students are going to fulfil their potential and be prepared for modern life.

In the common introduction to each of these chapters, we look at what the research says and the benefits and challenges of particular approaches. Each author then focuses on how to translate theory into practice in the context of their subject, offering practical lesson ideas and teacher tips. These chapters are not mutually exclusive but can be read independently of each other and in whichever order suits you best. They form a coherent whole but are presented in such a way that you can dip into the book when and where it is most convenient for you to do so.

The final two chapters are common to all the books in this series and are not written by the subject authors. After the subject context chapters, we include guidance on how to reflect on your teaching and some avenues you might explore to develop your own professional learning. Schools and educational organisations are increasingly interested in the impact that classroom practice has on student outcomes. We have therefore included an exploration of this topic and some practical advice on how to evaluate the success of the learning opportunities you are providing for your students.

We hope you find these books accessible and useful. We have tried to make them conversational in tone so you feel we are sharing good practice rather than directing it. Above all, we hope that the books will inspire you and enable you to think in more depth about how you teach and how your students learn.

Paul Ellis and Lauren Harris

Series Editors

2 | Purpose and context

International research into educational effectiveness tells us that student achievement is influenced most by what teachers do in classrooms. In a world of rankings and league tables we tend to notice performance, not preparation, yet the product of education is more than just examinations and certification. Education is also about the formation of effective learning habits that are crucial for success within and beyond the taught curriculum.

The purpose of this series of books is to inspire you as a teacher to reflect on your practice, try new approaches and better understand how to help your students learn. We aim to help you develop your teaching so that your students are prepared for the next level of their education as well as life in the modern world.

This book will encourage you to examine the processes of learning and teaching, not just the outcomes. We will explore a variety of teaching strategies to enable you to select which is most appropriate for your students and the context in which you teach. When you are making your choice, involve your students: all the ideas presented in this book will work best if you engage your students, listen to what they have to say, and consistently evaluate their needs.

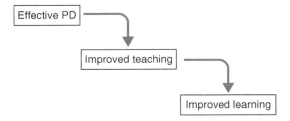

Cognitive psychologists, coaches and sports writers have noted how the aggregation of small changes can lead to success at the highest level. As teachers, we can help our students make marginal gains by guiding them in their learning, encouraging them to think and talk about how they are learning, and giving them the tools to monitor their success. If you take care of the learning, the performance will take care of itself.

When approaching an activity for the first time, or revisiting an area of learning, ask yourself if your students know how to:

- approach a new task and plan which strategies they will use
- monitor their progress and adapt their approach if necessary
- look back and reflect on how well they did and what they might do differently next time.

2 Approaches to learning and teaching Literature in English

Effective students understand that learning is an active process. We need to challenge and stretch our students and enable them to interrogate, analyse and evaluate what they see and hear. Consider whether your students:

- challenge assumptions and ask questions
- try new ideas and take intellectual risks
- devise strategies to overcome any barriers to their learning that they encounter.

As we discuss in Chapter 6 **Active learning** and Chapter 8 **Metacognition**, it is our role as teachers to encourage these practices with our students so that they become established routines. We can help students review their own progress as well as getting a snapshot ourselves of how far they are progressing by using some of the methods we explore in Chapter 7 on **Assessment for Learning**.

Students often view the subject lessons they are attending as separate from each other, but they can gain a great deal if we encourage them to take a more holistic appreciation of what they are learning. This requires not only understanding how various concepts in a subject fit together, but also how to make connections between different areas of knowledge and how to transfer skills from one discipline to another. As our students successfully integrate disciplinary knowledge, they are better able to solve complex problems, generate new ideas and interpret the world around them.

In order for students to construct an understanding of the world and their significance in it, we need to lead students into thinking habitually about why a topic is important on a personal, local and global scale. Do they realise the implications of what they are learning and what they do with their knowledge and skills, not only for themselves but also for their neighbours and the wider world? To what extent can they recognise and express their own perspective as well as the perspectives of others? We will consider how to foster local and global awareness, as well as personal and social responsibility, in Chapter 12 on **Global thinking**.

As part of the learning process, some students will discover barriers to their learning: we need to recognise these and help students to overcome them. Even students who regularly meet success face their own challenges. We have all experienced barriers to our own learning at some point in our lives and should be able as teachers to empathise and share our own methods for dealing with these.

In Chapter 10 **Inclusive education** we discuss how to make learning accessible for everyone and how to ensure that all students receive the instruction and support they need to succeed as students.

Some students are learning through the medium of English when it is not their first language, while others may struggle to understand subject jargon even if they might otherwise appear fluent. For all students, whether they are learning through their first language or an additional language, language is a vehicle for learning. It is through language that students access the content of the lesson and communicate their ideas. So, as teachers, it is our responsibility to make sure that language isn't a barrier to learning. In Chapter 9 on **Language awareness** we look at how teachers can pay closer attention to language to ensure that all students can access the content of a lesson.

Alongside a greater understanding of what works in education and why, we (as teachers) can also seek to improve how we teach and expand the tools we have at our disposal. For this reason, we have included Chapter 11 **Teaching with digital technologies**, discussing what this means for our classrooms and for us as teachers. Institutes of higher education and employers want to work with students who are effective communicators and who are information literate. Technology brings both advantages and challenges and we invite you to reflect on how to use it appropriately.

This book has been written to help you think harder about the impact of your teaching on your students' learning. It is up to you to set an example for your students and to provide them with opportunities to celebrate success, learn from failure and, ultimately, to succeed.

We hope you will share what you gain from this book with other teachers and that you will be inspired by the ideas that are presented here. We hope that you will encourage your school leaders to foster a positive environment that allows both you and your students to meet with success and to learn from mistakes when success is not immediate. We hope too that this book can help in the creation and continuation of a culture where learning and teaching are valued and through which we can discover together what works best for each and every one of our students.

3 | The nature of the subject

Why study Literature?

In my personal life and in my work as a teacher, literature provides me with inspiration, entertainment, insight and a retreat from the difficulties of life. You may also feel that literature is an important part of your life. However, your students may not share your view! In contrast, they probably see many practical advantages in the study of English Language. Most of these advantages are likely to relate to occupational choice and opportunity. The ability to read, speak and write in English is part of a set of skills demanded by the increasing globalisation of scholarship, business and politics. There are other advantages, of course: in social relationships, cultural development and self-esteem. However, a principal motivation for studying English Language is likely to be functionally related to accreditation for work and further study.

In contrast, the advantages of studying English Literature may seem less obvious. This is particularly true of students who find additional linguistic challenge in texts that do not conform to familiar models of functional English. They may not see the subject as relevant to their occupational choice and opportunity. They may even see Literature as unnecessarily 'artistic' or unproductive. It is worth challenging these notions.

What are the advantages of studying English Literature?

There are many, including the following:

1 Understanding human behaviour

Studying Literature widens the reader's experience of human behaviour and its origins in ideas, feelings and attitudes. Reading fiction set in different times and different cultures extends understanding of two vital aspects of humanity:

- firstly – how some human behaviours and motivations differ according to time, culture or circumstance
- secondly – and perhaps more importantly – how some human behaviours and motivations are the **same** across time and space.

(This may be called the 'vicarious experience' view of Literature study.)

2 Developing academic skills

Studying Literature develops academic skills, which match and contribute to skills in other subjects. It involves conveying understanding, classifying knowledge, investigating and evaluating evidence. It also involves speaking and writing relevantly, coherently and with precision. *(This may be called the 'transferable skills' view of Literature study.)*

3 Personal development

Studying Literature develops personal qualities of empathy with other people and insight into other situations. It provides a maturing of emotional intelligence through reflection and comparison. It also develops better understanding of oneself by comparison with others making choices and facing experiences in fiction. *(This may be called the 'personal growth and enrichment' view of Literature study.)*

4 Stimulating imagination

Studying Literature provides a recreational escape into other worlds. It works on and encourages imagination, and can be a stimulus to creativity – in life, conversation and in writing. It confers membership of a cultured community that is larger than the functional communities around. *(This may be called the 'cultural' view of Literature study.)*

5 Understanding communication

Studying Literature develops skill in understanding the principal medium of human communication – language. This is a key skill in work and leisure, applicable to the student's own language and the languages of others. It promotes a respect for effective language use and an ability to spot language that is being used to conceal, mislead or represent events in a biased way. *(This may be called the 'citizenship' view of Literature study.)*

What kind of study?

Your students will have different abilities, motivations and preferences, as well as distinctly individual personalities. You will want to choose study methods that engage all of your students, especially if you want to vary the activity to keep them engaged through a whole lesson or series of lessons. For example:

- You may choose to vary tasks and activities between solo, group and whole-class study.
- You may prescribe a sequence and focus of study or let them arrive at their own, choosing between directed and undirected study.

- You may choose to differentiate between different individuals or groups by implementing supported or independent study.
- You may choose to prompt their study, or to present the results of their study through speaking and listening and/or writing.

What kind of learning?

Any academic subject involves subject-specific **knowledge**. In Literature, this may include knowledge of plot and character, themes and ideas. It may involve technical terms such as genre, text structure and language for effect, or literary terms such as sonnet, novella or melodrama. In Literature study, knowledge is a basic requirement: however, it is what the student *does* with the knowledge that matters.

Therefore, in Literature study, the student's **response** matters, whether it is presented in academic terms or in terms of personal preference. Clearly, you will want to develop that response so that it benefits from learned skills of **analysis** as the basis of arriving at developed **interpretation**, or **evaluation** of different interpretations through **argument**. And throughout this you will want students to be learning that effective Literature study involves **comparison** of texts, writers and ideas, and an awareness of feelings and attitudes both within the students themselves and expressed in what they read.

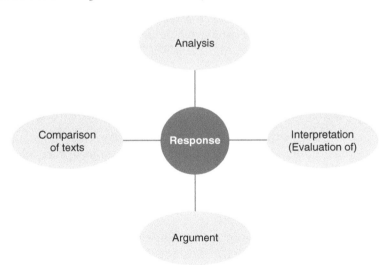

Figure 3.1: The student's response.

(Note: definitions of terms in bold blue can be found in the online glossary)

11

Teacher Tip

Response can be entirely personal but always gains from support with developed skills. The simplest way to develop a supported and developed response is to use appropriate terms. For example:

Response – I think, I feel
Analysis – The use of words such as 'xx' and 'xx' reveals that...
Interpretation – This may mean/could mean... It could also mean...
Evaluation – This is important because...
Comparison – Both texts... Similarly...

What kind of teaching?

As an English Literature teacher, you will operate in a number of different roles as you manage, motivate and develop your students.

- **Instructor.** Sometimes, when imparting information, you will be **instructing**. In this role you will be the authority whose information must be followed. This is a limited role in Literature study, as instruction is most appropriate to content features such as facts and to procedural features such as task-setting and processing.
- **Motivator.** Because you are dealing with human beings, contents and procedures are not automatically accepted, so you will need skills in **motivating**. These skills may involve encouragement and praise, and be individualised or group-orientated, as in competition. Skilful motivating needs to take into account the differences in ability in your class, so **stimulating** students who need less support and those who need more requires subtlety and adaptability in **differentiating** tasks and feedback.
- **Demonstrator.** All abilities will be helped when they see you demonstrate what they need to do, so **modelling** becomes an important role.
- **Monitor.** As your students work through the activities you have designed, you will adopt a **monitoring** role as you check on individuals' difficulties, progress and success.

- **Navigator.** Some tasks may be complex and take time, so you will need to be steering students in the right direction, **navigating** their progress through an individual lesson or the whole course.
- **Facilitator.** Where you have chosen to set students a task involving individualised discovery or group work, you will be setting up support resources and reference points, **facilitating** their independence rather than instructing or directing them.

Finally, and most importantly, you will be exploiting a skill in **questioning**, and following up any responses to your questions with feedback, which could involve personal responses, professional assessments or further questions in the process known as **dialoguing**. See Chapter 6 **Active learning** for more on these parts of the teacher's craft.

The four components of Literature study

Scholars and critics offer various sophisticated and complex explanations of what is involved in Literature study. Many are valid and interesting, but few are of use to secondary-level students. As a teacher, I need an explanation that works for and with my students, and in a way that supports effective classroom practice – hence my model of the four components of the 'world of Literature' study.

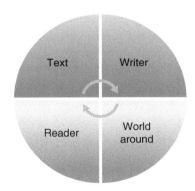

Figure 3.2: The four components of Literature study.

The four parts, or components, are fairly simple, though each can be developed as students become secure and more ambitious. It is helpful for students to see that these four parts are of equal importance. It is particularly important that they see themselves as active readers rather than passive receivers of texts: the individual student's personal responses matter more in Literature study than in some other subjects. The class may acquire the same **knowledge**, but attainment is **differentiated** by the way that individual students **apply** and **develop** that knowledge.

Literature is mainly divided into the three genres of poetry, prose and drama. All of these may be written to express a writer's interests, passions or obsessions, or to appeal to an audience paying to be entertained. The main difference is that most prose and poetry is read in private for enjoyment, insight or new experience. Drama is written for public performance, and interpreted by directors and actors before audiences have their chance to interpret it, while poetry and prose tend to be interpreted by readers on their own.

Writer

The **writer**'s ingredients for a text:

- **experiences:** describing memories, places, events, situations and people.
- **ideas:** proposing or opposing common notions, concepts or opinions.
- **feelings:** exploring the causes and effects of grief, love, anger, fear, joy, etc.
- **attitudes:** illustrating ways in which ideas, feelings and attitudes can be organised as a habitual posture for dealing with experiences.

⊡ LESSON IDEA ONLINE 3.1: EXPLORING KEY TERMS: IDEAS, FEELINGS AND ATTITUDES

Students may not have a clear understanding of the important differences between these three terms. This lesson idea is designed to help them explore the differences.

Reader

The **reader**'s ingredients for responding to a text:

- **experiences:** their own memories, places, events, situations and people.
- **ideas:** their own notions, concepts or opinions.
- **feelings:** emotions such as grief, love, anger, fear and joy.
- **attitudes:** their own habitual stance when dealing with experiences.

So, we can see that readers bring with them a lot of their own assumptions, beliefs and experiences that affect their responses to a text. Reading is not a passive 'soaking up' of ideas into an empty vessel. The best reading involves a connection of the reader's own experience, ideas, feelings and attitudes with those expressed by the author or illustrated by the author's text.

☑ LESSON IDEA ONLINE 3.2: IDEAS, ATTITUDES AND FEELINGS IN POETRY

Some poems are stronger on feelings than they are on ideas or attitudes. Others are stronger on attitudes than ideas. Students need to be able to see how these three ingredients may show themselves in poems. This lesson idea will allow them to explore this using 'Last Lesson of the Afternoon', by D.H. Lawrence.

Teacher Tip

Support students to develop their questioning skills, both individually and as a group:

1 Develop a focused questioning repertoire to develop **class** or **group** responses. Give your students a statement, then ask a group of three to respond with a) feelings, b) ideas, c) attitudes. For example:
   - 'Women are more intelligent than men.'
   - 'Science is more of a danger than a help.'
   - 'Teachers should be paid twice as much.'
2 Using these statements, develop a focused questioning repertoire to develop **individual** responses. Give one student a statement and ask him/her to respond with a) feelings, b) ideas, c) attitudes.

Approaches to learning and teaching Literature in English

True, the **texts** selected for literary study are the starting point, but the **reader**'s response to the text is just as important. Teachers know the texts very well, but want to know *what they mean to the readers*. Understanding why the **writer** chose to write this **text**, and what circumstances affected the **writer** at the time of writing, is also important in Literature study. Fitting all this into the **world around**, the context of other communications, ideas and experiences, makes Literature a part of life as a whole.

☑ LESSON IDEA ONLINE 3.3: IDEAS, ATTITUDES AND FEELINGS IN PROSE

Use this lesson idea to help students distinguish between ideas, attitudes and feelings, and to relate them to fiction.

☑ LESSON IDEA ONLINE 3.4: IDEAS, ATTITUDES AND FEELINGS IN DRAMA

Use this lesson idea to help students distinguish between ideas, attitudes and feelings, and to relate them to drama.

Text

The main features students need to understand about a text are:

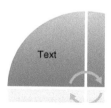

- conventions of the form (prose/poetry/drama)
- ways in which the structure within the form reflects the writer's craft and choices
- ways in which language is exploited to convey ideas, feelings and attitudes, and to influence these in the reader.

World around

The main features of the text's relationship to the world around are:

- influences of the world around at the time of writing
- ways in which the text has had an influence on the world around it, then and since
- ways in which the text has significance in the current world around
- any contexts in which the text takes new forms of presentation.

Teacher Tip

Use a questioning strategy to support students towards a focused and structured response.

1 Develop a focused set of questions to support a rounded response by asking an individual student questions based on the four components of the 'world of Literature' study.
   • What are the three most important words in the text?
   • As a reader, what strikes you as interesting or hard to understand?
   • What sort of person do you imagine the writer to be?
   • What would different kinds of readers think about this text?
2 Develop a focused set of questions to support a rounded response by asking a group of four students the same questions based on the four components of the 'world of Literature' study.

Developing a response repertoire

As you develop students' responses on the four-part 'world of Literature' study model, remind them that they will not always need to start with the **text**: they may prefer or find it more useful to start with the **reader**. The four parts can be rotated as necessary – and will not always be equally important. What matters is that students are allowed flexibility in their use of a structure for their response. The rest of this book will show how this set of responses can be applied and developed.

Summary

In this chapter you have looked at the range of subject coverage in Literature, divided into four key components. When considering the nature of English Literature, remember that:

• there are important distinctions between ideas, feelings and attitudes in the writer and in the reader

• Literature can be placed in the wider contexts of a student's own life and in the world around

• it is important to support students' confidence as readers.

4 | Key considerations

Teachers' subject knowledge

As an English teacher, you will have specialist subject knowledge that may be stronger in some aspects than in others. For example, some of us are more confident in our subject knowledge of grammatical and lexical aspects of language. Some are more confident in their subject knowledge of literature, while others are more confident in their knowledge of poetry, or the novel, or of drama. Whatever your own strengths, everything that you teach will need to be framed by the requirements of your syllabus. That will establish the content coverage of your Literature course.

In English Literature, this will involve a choice from a number of set texts. You will either choose according to what you already know, or something you have not previously read but which you think will be well suited to the needs and abilities of your students. Your teaching will also need to be framed by the assessment model that will measure your students' performance. This may involve external examinations or coursework. It may involve questions of studied set texts or questions on unseen texts. In all cases, you will need to be familiar with the criteria for the particular mode of assessment. These criteria will be generally stated in the assessment objectives and specifically organised in levels of attainment that show how your students' work will be assessed.

Students' subject knowledge

Many students may not be in the habit of reading literature, or reading literature in English. Their knowledge may be restricted to a general grasp of plot and character rather than **contexts** and features of literary genre and language. They will be helped by some introduction through screen and other media versions of their texts. Some sampling of short extracts to engage interest and highlight key features of the whole text can also be useful.

The four components of Literature study

All of these components direct your own knowledge and help you organise your own teaching. This ensures that what your students learn is appropriate to the requirements of their syllabus. The components help to give subject-specific detail to the general idea of a world of English Literature.

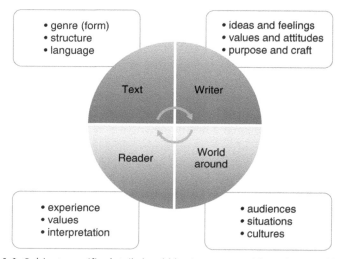

Figure 4.1: Subject-specific detail should be incorporated into the 'world of English Literature' model.

As we saw in Chapter 3, this model of the 'world of Literature' is a useful basis for students' learning focus and for your teaching focus. You can use it to set an agenda for a particular lesson, or for phases within a lesson. You can use it as the basis for a set of questions that ensures your students are familiar with anything they are likely to be asked in an examination.

Let's see how the model can be used to explore the subject-specialist knowledge and skills considered more generally in Chapter 3.

The text

Form and structure

The **form** (or genre) is usually a traditional text type inherited by the writer and used as a template, such as a sonnet which has 14 lines and a choice of 3 or 4 rhyme schemes. **Structure** is more interesting: it's the framework the writer creates within the form, and the skeleton, muscles and organs of the piece working together.

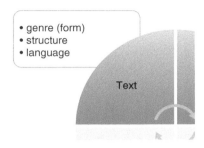

- genre (form)
- structure
- language

Text

Think of form as a silhouette – an outline of the shape of something.	Think of structure as what can be seen in an X-ray.

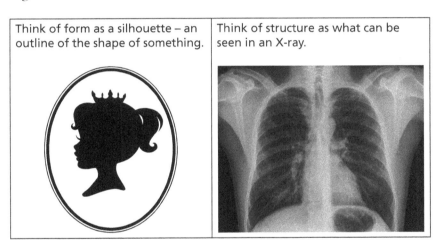

Figure 4.2: Form and structure.

☑ LESSON IDEA ONLINE 4.1: WORKING WITH KEY TERMS: FORM AND STRUCTURE IN POETRY

This lesson idea uses the *cinquain* form to clarify the difference between form and structure as literary terms. This can be helpful to students in structuring their own writing.

Teacher Tip

Check that students know the difference between form and structure: the form is inherited and traditional; the structure is what the writer does within the form.

For example, the form of a *cinquain* is lines of 2, 4, 6, 8, 2 syllables. The structure can be of one, two, three or four sentences, or two statements and a question, or a feeling, an idea then an attitude.

Choose an example from the *cinquains* provided in Lesson idea 4.1. Does it obey the rules of form? Does it show any variation in sentences or in sequence of ideas/feelings/attitudes?

Language

As all of the types of literature your students are likely to study are made up of language, it may seem obvious to state that the type of language used in a text is important, but it is worth examining this further. Here we look at three types of language that serve important functions in English Literature.

1 In a **Standard English text**, the language chosen is the clearest medium for communicating the content. For example, it is likely to be used where it is functionally relevant to the task of **narrative** explanation or giving information.

Teacher Tip

Language – **Standard English text**

Ask your students to select details from the opening of Jane Austen's *Pride and Prejudice* that make it, in their view, a Standard English text. An example is supplied here.

Original:

It is a truth universally acknowledged, that a single man in possession of a good fortune, must be in want of a wife.

Revision to Standard English:

However little known the feelings or views of such a man may be on his first entering a neighbourhood, this truth is

---

so well fixed in the minds of the surrounding families, that
he is considered the rightful property of one or other of
their daughters.

2   **Dialect** is used in literature to establish a character's distinctive social
or regional background.

Teacher Tip

Language – **Dialect**

Ask your students to identify dialect features in John
Agard's poem 'Half-Caste'. Consider diction, grammar and
pronunciation.

☑ LESSON IDEA ONLINE 4.2: WORKING WITH KEY TERMS: DIALOGUE AND DIALECT IN PROSE

Lesson idea 4.2 offers a developed lesson plan around the use
of dialect in spoken English using Thomas Hardy's *Far from the
Madding Crowd*.

☑ LESSON IDEA ONLINE 4.3: WORKING WITH KEY TERMS: DIALOGUE, DIALECT AND PRONUNCIATION IN DRAMA

This lesson idea provides an example of contrasted forms of
spoken language in English using *Pygmalion*, by George Bernard
Shaw.

3   **Pattern** decribes the forms of language chosen as an instrument for
creative exploitation. For example, distorted grammatical patterns
and word order might be chosen to create rhyme and rhythm in
poetry. In prose, unusual or distorted patterns of words or sentences
may be used to create a particular effect.

Teacher Tip

Language – **Pattern**

Ask your students to identify literary use of language in this extract from *Bleak House*, by Charles Dickens:

> Fog everywhere. Fog up the river, where it flows among green aits and meadows; fog down the river, where it rolls defiled among the tiers of shipping and the waterside pollutions of a great (and dirty) city. Fog on the Essex marshes, fog on the Kentish heights. Fog creeping into the cabooses of collier-brigs; fog lying out on the yards and hovering in the rigging of great ships; fog drooping on the gunwales of barges and small boats. Fog in the eyes and throats of ancient Greenwich pensioners, wheezing by the firesides of their wards; fog in the stem and bowl of the afternoon pipe of the wrathful skipper, down in his close cabin; fog cruelly pinching the toes and fingers of his shivering little 'prentice boy on deck.

The writer

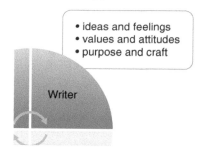

• ideas and feelings
• values and attitudes
• purpose and craft

Writer

Studying the text means studying what is finished and printed on the page. Think of that as the **content** – *what* the writer writes about. However, studying the writer goes beyond and behind the printed page. It is a matter of identifying what makes the writer distinctive and worth studying. It is also a matter of exploring the writer's **motivation** and **purpose**. This could be to entertain, to challenge, to illustrate or to explain.

Some writers are driven by a strong moral purpose. Others are driven by a need to record what they see as real life around them. And some writers are both. Think of that as the motivation – *why* the writer chooses to write.

Studying the writer is also a matter of appreciating the style of writing – the skill of constructing a text and using language to convey meaning. Think of that as the craft – *how* the writer writes.

☑ LESSON IDEA ONLINE 4.4: WORKING WITH KEY TERMS: STRUCTURE IN PROSE FICTION

Use this lesson idea to help students to see that a writer's craft can be seen in either consistency through a text, or in variety and contrast through a text, or in both.

☑ LESSON IDEA ONLINE 4.5: WORKING WITH KEY TERMS: NARRATIVE AND DIALOGUE IN PROSE FICTION

Use this lesson idea to help students see the authorial craft working in *Lord of the Flies*, by William Golding.

Teacher Tip

Ask your students to colour-code a sonnet according to the way it is organised into different ideas/feelings/attitudes. For example, try blue (cold colour) for ideas, red (warm colour) for feelings and perhaps green ('go ahead' sign) for attitudes.

The reader

As an English teacher, you will be your students' model of how to read. In its simplest sense, this means you will be able to read a passage aloud to them in a way that brings the text to life and engages their interest, their curiosity or their enthusiasm. Your students will also learn from you how to read for initial meaning, how to probe for implied meaning and how to read for authorial craft in aspects of language and structure. In order to build these skills within your students so that they become increasingly independent and confident, and ready to apply their skills in different contexts, you need to give them classroom practice in those skills.

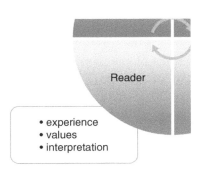

Reader

• experience
• values
• interpretation

The student reader needs to know that their teachers will be looking for more than understanding of what has been read. They will be looking for evidence of interpreting and evaluating what they have understood. This means that students' opinions of their texts matter. They need to have confidence in using their own experiences, their own thoughts and their own feelings in their response to literature – not just a literary response but a personal literary response also. Obviously, it will be an informed personal literary response because it will include knowledge and skills related to the study of literature, but it is important that students know that their personal engagement with texts is valued. As the teacher, you can model ways in which a personal response is meshed with an informed response.

LESSON IDEA 4.6: PRESENTING A PERSONAL LITERARY RESPONSE

Tell the class why you (the teacher) like a particular poem/novel/ play (personal preference) then why you think it is also relevant (ideas) and well-written (details of craft in language and structure). For example:

- relevant (ideas) – e.g. apt or interesting ideas on love, war, relationships, the state of the planet
- well-written (craft) – e.g. choice of words, use of dialogue, clever rhymes, apt and interesting similes/metaphors.

The world around

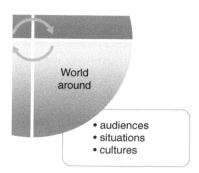

World around

- audiences
- situations
- cultures

This aspect of study and response requires more than understanding of the printed page. It requires an understanding of how the ideas, feelings, situations and characters of the text are relevant to readers in different times and in different places. It also relates to ways in which texts are reproduced or performed in contexts other than print on the page. This is particularly important in drama, where stage or screen performances may bring a text to an audience in various ways.

Developing key considerations

The four-part model of Literature study described in this chapter has four strong advantages:

- It ensures that your teaching and questioning are always clearly focused.
- It ensures that your students' learning is relevant to the syllabus.
- It places the reader on the same status as the writer and the text, giving full value to individualised personal response.
- It develops a reading discipline that helps students' reading in other subjects – and their reading and response to whatever they experience in life beyond formal education.

Summary

In this chapter we have looked at some of the key considerations when teaching English Literature. The chapter has provided the opportunity to extend your subject knowledge through looking at:

- text structure as a key feature of Literature study
- varieties of language within English.

It is important to remember:

- your role as a model of how to read literary texts
- that students respond as readers with their own ideas, attitudes and feelings.

5 | Interpreting a syllabus

Choosing a syllabus and planning your teaching

When you choose your Literature syllabus you will have various reasons for your choice. You may choose a syllabus because you have taught it before, and you want to stay with what is familiar. It may be that your school has always used the same syllabus and wants you to stay with it. These are teacher-focused and school-focused reasons for choice. You will also, I hope, consider how well the syllabus matches the specific needs, interests and abilities of your students.

This student-focused choice puts more emphasis on evaluating the syllabus for specific advantages in teaching and learning. The most important aspect of syllabus choice is the scope it gives you for enthusiasm in presenting texts that engage your students' interest. Your role as guide, director and manager of learning will be much easier if you feel that your text is something you care for and enjoy. Your enthusiasm is a vital prompt for your students' enthusiasm and understanding. Texts that make them laugh, and texts that deal with emotions and situations similar to those they have experienced, will give memorable life to your lessons.

Evaluating a syllabus with assessment in mind

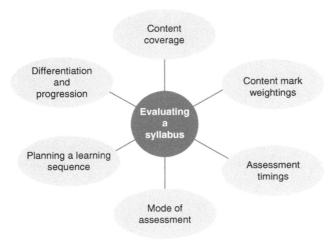

Figure 5.1: Key points when evaluating your syllabus.

5

Approaches to learning and teaching Literature in English

Content coverage

The syllabus will include coverage of the three main genres of Literature, with some choice in the set texts offered. Some set texts appear on many syllabuses but there may be other texts that particularly appeal to you. **Your preferences matter.** You need to choose texts that you can teach with enthusiasm, but you also need to be sure that they will be interesting and suitable for your students. There may be cultural reasons why some texts are not well suited to your students.

Teacher Tip

It doesn't always work to teach the texts you know best, or the ones that have suited previous students or students at another school. You could test students' interest and understanding by giving them an introductory sample of several texts.

Content mark weightings

Usually, all genres carry the same mark weighting, but some students may be more confident in one genre than in another. Similarly, some students will feel more confident with prose than they do with poetry. Your students will need to balance their time and effort across all three genres to demonstrate their best abilities.

Poetry can be studied in small units at various times, but plays and novels need to be studied in a continuous sequence. If your students are not confident in dealing with unfamiliar texts, you may choose to avoid a syllabus that has a substantial weighting on **unseen text** questions.

Some syllabuses have part-questions, with a fixed number of marks for each part. For example, a simple request to select and retrieve a word or fact may be worth only 1 or 2 marks. A more demanding part to evaluate two conflicting statements may require more thought, but will be worth more marks, so the time will be well spent.

Teacher Tip

Check example questions for the pattern of questioning and sequencing of response skills needed.

- You may find that some questions are easier 'settling in' questions. Later questions may be more demanding.
- Some questions may direct students to a specific part of a text.

Assessment timings

Students need to know how long to allow for different questions. It's a common fault to spend too long on the first few questions, leaving too little time for later questions or the last question, which is likely to offer the opportunity to demonstrate higher-level skills.

Mode of assessment

Check the range of assessment modes that your students are likely to encounter. These could include:

- **Multiple-choice questions**. These require much reading or writing, and allow some luck in choosing the right answer, but they don't usually carry many marks.
- **Closed-book questions**. These require response from memory.
- **Open-book questions**. These require the student to find appropriate material from the text.
- **Questions on previously unseen texts**. These require students to respond spontaneously.

You need to ensure that your students are confident in all of these assessment modes. Some questions use a format in which the first part is based on a given extract and the second part based on another extract of the student's choice.

Teacher Tip

Plan opportunities to practise a range of assessment modes. For example:

- multiple-choice tasks, such as 'Which of the following words in verse 1 show the writer's feelings? [haste, remember, anger, few]'
- 'select and retrieve' activities, such as 'Which words in verse 2 convey the writer's feelings of …?'

Planning a learning sequence

You need an overall plan for your students' learning experience that gradually increases the demands on their knowledge and understanding. Your plan also needs to give opportunities to assess how well their learning is going at various stages. Your course of study should allow your students to progress from a relatively unconfident first encounter through to more detailed study and use of an increasing range of cognitive and affective responses. Don't be afraid to go back to an earlier part of the text when students are more knowledgeable and confident, in order to see if their understanding and response have developed from the earlier encounter. You could do this by asking them if their later knowledge makes a difference to how a character was presented earlier, or if there were any clues to the way the plot was going to develop that they missed during the first time of reading.

Differentiation and progression

Some students need more support than others, for a variety of reasons. Where tasks and questions are matched to students' different abilities, this is referred to as **differentiation**. Be aware that even if the learning sequence is the same for all, the **progression** will vary between individuals. Some students may need tasks that consolidate their knowledge of plot, character or themes in parts of the text they have already studied, while others may need tasks that prompt them to read ahead or anticipate what may be ahead. See Chapter 8 **Metacognition** for ways in which progression involves competence in increasingly sophisticated concepts.

LESSON IDEA ONLINE 5.1: BASIC SKILL: SELECTION AND RETRIEVAL

This lesson idea focuses on developing the ability to **select and retrieve, explain, and interpret and analyse**.

LESSON IDEA ONLINE 5.2: INTERMEDIATE SKILL: EXPLANATION

This lesson idea focuses on developing the ability to **select, select and retrieve, explain, and interpret and analyse**.

LESSON IDEA ONLINE 5.3: DEVELOPED SKILL: INTERPRETATION AND ANALYSIS

This lesson idea focuses on developing the ability to **select, select and retrieve, explain, and interpret and analyse**, using a scene from *Romeo and Juliet*, by William Shakespeare.

Implementing a syllabus

All this needs to be planned according to the time allowed for your course. For instance:

- a one-year course is likely to emphasise specific main features of the text your students are studying
- a two-year course may give scope for broader and wider reading (e.g. of similar texts or of other texts by the author).

In many cases, a two-year course may be allocated by your school for the study of Language and Literature. You will need to decide whether to teach these consecutively or together.

Teacher Tip

Some skills in reading are common to English Language and Literature syllabuses, so it will make sense to plan some study including both, rather than thinking of the two courses as separate.

For example, both courses involve reading skills of interpretation of meaning and analysis of writer's methods, although the texts themselves may be different (e.g. fiction or non-fiction). Writers of both kinds of texts may use similes, metaphors, emotive words and varied sentence structures. Noticing these is equally important in reading for Language and for Literature.

Set texts and students' ability

You need to decide which set texts to choose for your students to study. The choice will depend upon students' needs and interests, but also upon their abilities. You may choose different texts for different classes. You may choose the same text for different classes, but differentiate according to ability in the kind of focus and questioning you use. For example:

- Those students with less developed English language skills may be doing well to get a grasp of the *who?*, *when?*, and *where?* aspects of a text. These will be focused on the plot, or the story.
- More able and ambitious students will need to tackle a more challenging focus and questioning based on the *why?* and the *how?*

You will also need to decide how much of the text you are going to read with them and study in class, and how much you will ask them to do independently. Those with less developed English language skills will have greater need of your classroom guidance.

Visual support for textual study

You may also choose to help students to familiarise themselves with a text by showing them a screen version. In this case, be aware that the version may have edited or additional features representing the director's interpretation, which may or may not be the same as the author's. This may confuse those students with less developed English language skills, but it is something that will prompt the more able students to higher levels of comparative, evaluative and analytical response. If seeing the screened version makes them familiar with plot, character and situation, then that's a help. However, you need to make sure they understand that they should respond to the written text and not to the film based on it.

Teacher Tip

Give your students practice in longer whole-question response, first orally, then in writing. For example:

- 'How far do the poems you have studied bring out different ideas about love/war?'
- 'How are the author's changing feelings indicated by the use of language throughout the poem?'

Use examples of different students' responses to show acceptable varieties of detail and interpretation.

It is worth remembering that a syllabus is designed to be an introduction to a potentially vast field of study. Students' experience of the literature in their syllabus may be their last educational contact with the subject, or it may lead them to further study at university. In either case, syllabus designers hope that all students will find an interest and pleasure in literature beyond the requirements of examinations. After all, literature is for life, not just for study!

Summary

In this chapter you have looked at the reasons for choosing a syllabus. The lesson ideas provide practical ways of applying and developing this guidance. You have begun to consider:

- the ways in which a syllabus assesses your students' performance with a focus on the specific demands of different assessment modes

- how to plan your course as a developmental study sequence.

As a result, your students' learning will be enhanced and they will be better prepared for assessment.

6 Active learning

What is active learning?

Active learning is a pedagogical practice that places student learning at its centre. It focuses on *how* students learn, not just on *what* they learn. We as teachers need to encourage students to 'think hard', rather than passively receive information. Active learning encourages students to take responsibility for their learning and supports them in becoming independent and confident learners in school and beyond.

Research shows us that it is not possible to transmit understanding to students by simply telling them what they need to know. Instead, we need to make sure that we challenge students' thinking and support them in building their own understanding. Active learning encourages more complex thought processes, such as evaluating, analysing and synthesising, which foster a greater number of neural connections in the brain. While some students may be able to create their own meaning from information received passively, others will not. Active learning enables all students to build knowledge and understanding in response to the opportunities we provide.

Why adopt an active learning approach?

We can enrich all areas of the curriculum, at all stages, by embedding an active learning approach.

In active learning, we need to think not only about the content but also about the process. It gives students greater involvement and control over their learning. This encourages all students to stay focused on their learning, which will often give them greater enthusiasm for their studies. Active learning is intellectually stimulating and taking this approach encourages a level of academic discussion with our students that we, as teachers, can also enjoy. Healthy discussion means that students are engaging with us as a partner in their learning.

Students will better be able to revise for examinations in the sense that revision really is 're-vision' of the ideas that they already understand.

Active learning develops students' analytical skills, supporting them to be better problem solvers and more effective in their application of knowledge. They will be prepared to deal with challenging and unexpected situations. As a result, students are more confident in continuing to learn once they have left school and are better equipped for the transition to higher education and the workplace.

What are the challenges of incorporating active learning?

When people start thinking about putting active learning into practice, they often make the mistake of thinking more about the activity they want to design than about the learning. The most important thing is to put the student and the learning at the centre of our planning. A task can be quite simple but still get the student to think critically and independently. Sometimes a complicated task does not actually help to develop the student's thinking or understanding at all. We need to consider carefully what we want our students to learn or understand and then shape the task to activate this learning.

Active *versus* passive reading

Many students think that the point of study is to draw information out of a text. This is a valid part of their development of reading skills, but it is not what matters most in English Literature. Drawing information out of a text is a one-way process. It makes the reader a passive recipient of the textual content. You need to help your students to be **active readers** rather than **passive readers**.

You can help them to develop active and independent learning by getting them used to discovering rather than receiving. You need to reverse the **instructor** relationship between teacher and student where the teacher knows and tells. You need to be the **facilitator** of their learning (see Chapter 3 **The nature of the subject**) and your students need to find out and tell you what they know.

Set students homework in which they have to find something for themselves that they can bring back to the class to share with you and other students. They will be happy to use the internet rather than look up the indexes of print volumes.

Some examples of facilitated or guided learning by discovery:

- Find out three major world events that occurred in the five years before the publication of a studied text.
- Find out how popular/successful a text was in its time by checking the history of reprints in the five years following publication.
- Find out how the chapters of *Great Expectations* were written by Charles Dickens for serial publication in his magazine *All the Year Round*.
- Find out from a given source a key idea related to an author's comments on his/her own work. For example:
  - In the Preface to the 1912 edition of the collected *Wessex Tales* novels, to which country did Thomas Hardy compare Wessex, and to which authors did he compare himself?
  - How did Jane Austen describe her own writing in a letter to James Austen on 16 December 1816?

This chapter will help you to encourage your students to learn by doing things themselves, rather than simply listening to you.

6

Interactive reading and focused questioning

In Literature study, it is important for students' responses to show they have **interacted** with the text. Interactive reading requires *thinking* about the reading and writing processes. Students need to move from 'What' questions about facts to 'Why' and 'How' questions about ideas, attitudes, feelings and the writer's craft.

Your students need practice in interactive reading: they need to get used to questioning or interrogating the text. This is where you can help them by modelling carefully focused questioning:

- The simplest questions to ask of a text are: 'What is its purpose?' and 'Who is it written for?'
- A more searching question is: 'What does the text reveal about the writer's attitudes, ideas, feelings and beliefs?' or 'Why do you think the writer chose this topic and this way of presenting it?'
- Another more searching question is one that focuses on the reader rather than the text: 'How does this text impact on me?' or 'How does this text relate to what's going on in the world around me?'
- And, of course, there is the Literature-specific searching question that is a mix of all of these questions: 'How has the writer structured this text and used language to appeal to and influence the reader?'

Questions based on the four components of Literature study

Students will benefit from having a repertoire of questions based on the model of English Literature illustrated in Chapter 3 The nature of the subject.

The four components of the 'world of Literature' study model is a simple way of ensuring that students become accustomed to a focus on all the Literature assessment objectives. It can be the basis for your dialogue with individual students, small groups of students or with the whole group. Questioning your students is important, especially when your questions are about more than basic knowledge and understanding.

Focused classroom questioning strategies

Sometimes your role as a teacher is to provide answers. At other times, your role is to ask questions. The focus of your questions needs to be varied so that they signal different kinds of responses in answer. You need a questioning strategy that goes beyond checking on their understanding or their attention.

Your students will soon realise that your questions are not just random if they follow a pattern. Here is a simple but effective pattern:

A single student can be made a more active learner by being asked four questions in a row based on the four components of the 'world of Literature' model. For example:

- **Text**: 'Can you find an example of a word which has an emotional effect in the first verse?'
- **Writer**: 'What does the writer's choice of that word suggest about his/her feelings, ideas or beliefs?'
- **Reader**: 'Has this use of language made you feel any emotion, or not?'
- **World around**: 'How might the writer's feelings expressed in that word be received by your parents/your teacher/your friends?'

Teacher Tip

The same pattern of questions can be used with a group of four students, with you explaining that there is a different focus required by each question. You can put the questions to them individually in turn, so that each one has his/her own task. Even better, because it is more active, you can allow them to discuss a group answer to each question through collaboration.

From instruction to discovery

Developing an active learning approach in your students has implications for the way you teach. If you tell them what to *think*, they won't need to think for themselves. If you are always *instructing* them, they are always going to be passively *receiving* what you tell them.

6

Approaches to learning and teaching Literature in English

So, your skill as a teacher is to develop strategies for students to discover for themselves what you could tell them. One simple strategy that can be for individuals, pairs or groups is **role-play**. This is well suited to making their discussion productive and their study collaborative.

Teacher Tip

You could ask an *individual student* to play the role of a character in a text (or the writer) and think aloud about some of the ideas, feelings and attitudes in the text.

They could do this from a prepared script written in class or for homework, or you could make it a 'hot-seating' exercise where you take the role of interviewer and ask them questions about their motives or intentions.

You could make this a *paired* exercise by asking another student to take the role of interviewer, putting questions about the character's/writer's background, motivation and hopes.

You could make it a *group* exercise by asking three students to take the role of interviewers from different magazines/ news outlets/interest groups, each asking the same questions.

☑ **LESSON IDEA ONLINE 6.1: SOUND AND SENSE IN POETRY**
This lesson develops appreciation of a writer's exploitation of vowels, rhythm, alliteration and assonance as devices in a poem to reproduce the sensations associated with a steam locomotive.

Four conditions for active learning

To promote active learning you need to be prepared to give students the right *conditions* for active learning. The right conditions will involve stepping back from your role as front-of-whole-class instructor.

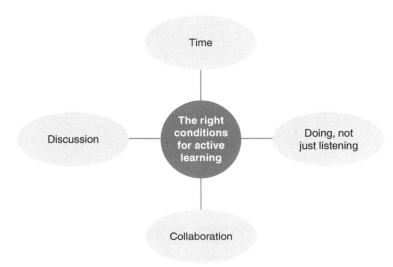

Figure 6.1: The right conditions for active learning.

Time

The first condition is that it will take students longer to arrive at an understanding than if you gave them the understanding. Your lessons need to build in time for them to work things out for themselves.

Teacher Tip

Help your students to make good use of timings. Give them practice in different time-allowances for different kinds of task. For example:

- 15 seconds for a simple 'select and retrieve' task
- one minute for an 'explain' ideas/feelings/attitudes task
- between three and five minutes for an 'interpret/analyse' task based on a large or whole part of the text (you could refer to the lesson ideas in Chapter 5 **Interpreting a syllabus** for exercise ideas).

Doing, not just listening

The second condition allows for physical and sensory involvement. The point of active learning is that the text is experienced more actively than in silent reading. You can use a visual and/or auditory stimulus, and the physical management of text. Some students may find it easier to represent their response to a text in a diagram, drawing or a compilation of visual images taken from digital sources. The essence of active learning is that it is more than listening or copying, and it usually involves doing something rather than simply reading something.

Teacher Tip

Set individuals/pairs/groups the task of converting a piece of drama script into prose as though in a novel. You could use an extract from *An Inspector Calls*, by J.B. Priestley. This will give them practice in managing the difference between dialogue and reported speech.

LESSON IDEA ONLINE 6.2: LANGUAGE AND CHARACTERISATION IN PROSE FICTION

The emphasis in this lesson is on the way Charles Dickens uses verbs to convey Mrs Joe's force and precision as she performs a simple kitchen routine.

LESSON IDEA ONLINE 6.3: CREATING DIRECTOR'S NOTES

This lesson illustrates how text is made more meaningful through movement by creating director's notes to help an actor perform an extract of drama script from *An Inspector Calls* by J.B. Priestley. As an alternative you could also use an excerpt from *A Raisin in the Sun* by Lorraine Hansberry.

Collaboration

The third condition is **allowed cooperation**. There is less pressure on students when they can tell each other that they don't understand something than admitting it to a teacher or the whole class. Working together helps students to learn together. They do this by sharing problems and sharing ideas, sometimes finding different knowledge and understanding in a partner. Even more valuably, they may find different interpretations of the same knowledge and understanding.

Teacher Tip

Sometimes it helps if you give individuals in a group specific roles and responsibilities. For example, you could make one the chair or task manager, keeping talk focused on the agenda; another the note-taker; another the person who reports back to the rest of the class.

☑ LESSON IDEA ONLINE 6.4: TEXT TRANSFORMATION

This lesson idea emphasises the language register associated with different text types, and the difference between the language of literature and the language of news media.

Discussion

The fourth condition is acceptance of discussion, or talk, as part of the learning process. Collaboration can be silent, but there is little point in that. Students working things out for themselves will likely need talk-time, some of which may not seem to be completely on-task. Do not be afraid to have some noise of discussion in your class. You can manage this noise by ensuring a clear focus for the discussion is maintained, and by setting a time for it to result in some feedback to you and the class.

☑ LESSON IDEA ONLINE 6.5: ENGAGING WITH ACTIVE LEARNING IN THE CLASSROOM

Use this lesson idea to engage your students with active learning in the classroom.

Obviously, your role as a teacher is to take overall responsibility for your students' learning. However, if all learning is dictated by you as the teacher, your students are unlikely to develop as independent learners. Giving students some responsibility for their own learning will help them to be effective discoverers rather than effective receivers. The activities in this chapter help your students to learn by *doing*, rather than by *listening*. Active classrooms make active learners – and make you active as an organiser, observer and assessor.

Summary

In this chapter you have:

- considered ways in which your role as a teacher is to create opportunities for students to learn for themselves by being more actively engaged with their tasks and with each other

- understood the importance of talk between students and the importance of preparing questioning routines that vary the demand and focus of learning.

Assessment
for Learning

What is Assessment for Learning?

Assessment for Learning (AfL) is a teaching approach that generates feedback that can be used to improve students' performance. Students become more involved in the learning process and, from this, gain confidence in what they are expected to learn and to what standard. We as teachers gain insights into a student's level of understanding of a particular concept or topic, which helps to inform how we support their progression.

We need to understand the meaning and method of giving purposeful feedback to optimise learning. Feedback can be informal, such as oral comments to help students think through problems, or formal, such as the use of rubrics to help clarify and scaffold learning and assessment objectives.

Why use Assessment for Learning?

By following well-designed approaches to AfL, we can understand better how our students are learning and use this to plan what we will do next with a class or individual students (see Figure 7.1). We can help our students to see what they are aiming for and to understand what they need to do to get there. AfL makes learning visible; it helps students understand more accurately the nature of the material they are learning and themselves as learners. The quality of interactions and feedback between students and teachers becomes critical to the learning process.

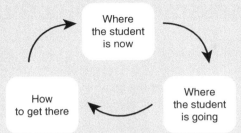

Figure 7.1: How can we use this plan to help our students?

We can use AfL to help our students focus on specific elements of their learning and to take greater responsibility for how they might move forward. AfL creates a valuable connection between assessment and learning activities, as the clarification of objectives will have a direct impact on how we devise teaching and learning strategies. AfL techniques can support students in becoming more confident in what they are learning, reflective in how they are learning, more likely to try out new approaches, and more engaged in what they are being asked to learn.

What are the challenges of incorporating AfL?

The use of AfL does not mean that we need to test students more frequently. It would be easy to just increase the amount of summative assessment and use this formatively as a regular method of helping us decide what to do next in our teaching. We can judge how much learning has taken place through ways other than testing, including, above all, communicating with our students in a variety of ways and getting to know them better as individuals.

The assessment objectives

Some teachers think of assessment as something that happens at the *end* of the teaching and learning process. This is a mistake. You need to use the assessment criteria as signposts and targets *throughout* your course. They need to be embedded in your daily teaching and in your questioning repertoire.

Your students' learning will be more focused and successful if it is developed in line with the criteria used to judge it. This means they need to be aware of the assessment objectives, and you need to use them **diagnostically** and **formatively** throughout the teaching and learning process. In short, you need to use assessment *for* learning as well as assessment *of* learning.

This means that you need to feed back to students, verbally or in writing, comments that help them to see where they are working purposefully towards an assessment objective, or where they seem to be ignoring an assessment objective. Such feedback during the process is more helpful to them than a summative grade put on their work at the end of the process.

Literature assessment objectives

The **assessment objectives** (AOs), for example as shown in the Cambridge IGCSE® English Literature syllabus (0486), may seem fairly straightforward.

- **AO1.** Show detailed knowledge of the content of literary texts in the three main forms (drama, poetry and prose), supported by reference to the text.
- **AO2.** Understand the meanings of literary texts and their contexts, and explore texts beyond surface meanings to show deeper awareness of ideas and attitudes.
- **AO3.** Recognise and appreciate ways in which writers use language, structure and form to create and shape meanings and effects.
- **AO4.** Communicate a sensitive and informed personal response to literary texts.

However, to make the assessment objectives come to life in the classroom, you need to see the separate skills that are embedded in them. This will enable you to decide which skills individual students need to work on, so that you don't set the same task for all students, including those who have already acquired the skill. It will also help you and your students to see that some skills are more complex than others. These more complex skills are more highly rewarded.

Using assessment objectives to build students' reading skills

Although the assessment objectives are designed for all students, it is clear that they represent two main levels of response. See the differences between basic and developed skills in this chart.

Basic skills	Developed skills
Knowledge of content supported by reference to the text	***Detailed knowledge*** of content supported by reference to the text
Understand surface meanings and contexts	***Explore*** for deeper awareness of ideas and attitudes
Recognise ways in which writers use language, structure and form to create and shape meanings and effects	***Appreciate*** ways in which language structure and form shape meanings and effects
Personal response to texts	***Sensitive and informed*** personal response

Table 7.1: The hierarchy of Literature reading skills.

You will be able to see from this which of your students need practice in the basic skills (knowledge and understanding) before they move on to the developed skills (explore and appreciate). Most students will be able to make a simple personal response to texts, but they will need your help to *develop* that response (sensitive and informed).

If students know how their work will be assessed, they will be able to focus their responses on the key skills being assessed. They can be helped to do this in two ways:

- by applying the criteria to their own writing – i.e. self-assessment.
- by working in pairs to apply the criteria to each other's work – i.e. peer-assessment.

Peer-assessment

Peer-assessment has three features valuable to teachers and students:

- It makes students familiar with the criteria by which their work will eventually be assessed.
- It allows students to compare their work and identify strengths and weaknesses informally in English or their own first language.

- It gives teachers a valuable opportunity to listen to students talk and assess their understanding of the work and of the syllabus focus and criteria.

LESSON IDEA ONLINE 7.1: MAKING SENSE OF THE KEY SKILLS – CRITICAL COMMENT ON POETRY

This lesson aims to help students see the difference between descriptive comment and critical comment by using examples of students' writing about Simon Armitage's poem, 'The Manhunt'.

LESSON IDEA ONLINE 7.2: MAKING SENSE OF THE KEY SKILLS – CRITICAL COMMENT ON PROSE FICTION

This lesson gives examples of descriptive and critical responses that show some active critical focus on *Of Mice and Men*, by John Steinbeck.

LESSON IDEA ONLINE 7.3: MAKING SENSE OF THE KEY SKILLS – CRITICAL COMMENT ON DRAMA

This lesson uses questions to prompt students to give skill-specific responses to a short extract from Shakespeare's *Macbeth*.

LESSON IDEA ONLINE 7.4: MAKING SENSE OF THE KEY SKILLS – INTERPRETATION

This lesson provides practical activities to engage students with editing a Shakespearean text in order to present an interpretation for an audience.

The four components of Literature study

Think back to the the the four components of the 'world of Literature' study model (as discussed in Chapter 3 **The nature of the subject** and Chapter 4 **Key considerations**). It's not difficult to see how the specifics of Literature study (and the assessment objectives) fit into the four-part model. Figure 4.1 shows how to develop each part of the four components with more depth and detail.

Mark schemes

Most syllabus **mark schemes** use a similar set of key terms to indicate rungs on the ladder of attainment: These help you to assess and plan your students' progression according to a skills hierarchy of increasing demand:

- analyse (developed — higher)
- explore (developed — higher)
- interpret (developed — intermediate)
- explain (developed — intermediate)
- identify (basic)
- understand (basic).

(Bloom's Cognitive Taxonomy, covered in depth in Chapter 10 **Inclusive education**, is a useful tool to help develop cognitive responses, is. However, it does not account for the emotional, attitudinal, aesthetic and moral aspects of literary response, which is why De Bono's approach is a better model for developing skills in literary reading.)

If you look at the basic skills embedded in the assessment objectives ('understand and identify'), you will know which of your students need practice in these before they can make further progress. Your students need to know what they can do now and what they need to do next.

Teacher Tip

Ask your students to work with key terms. Which of these is **understand** and which is **identify**?

1 *The writer uses language to express his feelings.*
2 *When he describes his feelings he uses similes and metaphors.*

The middle level of skills, 'explain and interpret', require more active reading (as discussed in Chapter 6 **Active learning**). Explaining does more than just select and retrieve an appropriate example. By prompting your students to explain more complex ideas such as use of language or feelings they begin to interpret the text, developing an active relationship with the text.

Teacher Tip

Using 'Last Lesson of the Afternoon', by D.H. Lawrence, ask your students to work with key terms. Which of these is **identify** and which is **explain**?

1 *The phrase 'like a pack of unruly hounds' is a simile.*
2 *Referring to his students with the simile 'like a pack of unruly hounds' shows that he thinks of them as badly behaved and like animals.*

If you work on students' ability to explain, you can develop explanations of more than literal meanings of words or parts of the text. Explaining can be simple explanation of meaning, but you can prompt your students to provide more complex explanations by asking them to explain purpose, audience, ideas, attitudes, feelings, effects, motivations or use of language. This is where explaining turns into a more personal and active relationship with texts, called interpreting.

Teacher Tip

Using 'Last Lesson of the Afternoon', by D.H. Lawrence, ask your students to work with key terms. Which of these is **explain** and which is **interpret**?

1 *Referring to his students with the simile 'like a pack of unruly hounds' shows that he thinks of them as badly behaved and like animals.*
2 *The way he refers to his students as 'unruly hounds' makes me think he has failed to keep them in order and he may not be a successful teacher.*

Interpretation tends to be more personal and active than explanation, and it needs confidence in personal judgement. You can build your students' confidence by reminding them that sometimes there is no single 'correct' interpretation in Literature study. There are perhaps as many interpretations as there are readers. Your students need to be able to try out – risk – an interpretation even if they are not sure about it. This tentative approach to possible interpretation will be helped by supporting arguments, but the main thing is that it *explores*. Exploring sometimes means venturing. Exploring and venturing may not always result in arrival at an intended destination, but they can be interesting along the way.

Teacher Tip

Using 'Last Lesson of the Afternoon', by D.H. Lawrence, ask your students to work with key terms. Which of these is **interpret** and which is **explore**?

1 *The way he refers to his students as 'unruly hounds' makes me think he has failed to keep them in order and he may not be a successful teacher.*
2 *If his pupils behave like 'unruly hounds' it may be because they are very badly behaved and hard to control, but it could mean that he does not seem in control and they have lost respect for his authority.*

The best explorers use a map and compass, and have a strong sense of where they want to go, but they are bold enough to value the journey for its own sake and sometimes get off the recommended path or ignore the established footpaths. What makes this kind of textual exploration a secure academic activity is when it is supported by a careful assembling of evidence to show that the journey has resulted in a clear understanding of the territory explored. This assembling of evidence is what we call analysis.

Teacher Tip

Get your students to work with key terms. Which of these is **explore** and which is **analyse**?

1 *If his pupils behave like 'unruly hounds' it may be because they are very badly behaved and hard to control, but it could mean that he does not seem in control and they have lost respect for his authority.*

2 *Throughout the poem there are details of what he has been trying to cope with: 'dross of indifference', 'insults' and 'slovenly work'. The effect on him is to make him 'sick, and tired', 'working weariedly' until he has used up his 'last dear fuel'. The effort to teach them has left him exhausted and has destroyed his motivation.*

Summary

In this chapter you have looked at how to integrate key skills related to the assessment objectives into your classroom practice. Assessment is not something at the end of the teaching and learning process, but something within the teaching and learning process. Remember that:

• assessment is *for* learning as well as *of* learning

• there is a hierarchy of skills for literary reading

• you need to place these skills within the wider context of English as a humane discipline – using the four components of the 'world of Literature' study model.

Metacognition

8

What is metacognition?

Metacognition describes the processes involved when students plan, monitor, evaluate and make changes to their own learning behaviours. These processes help students to think about their own learning more explicitly and ensure that they are able to meet a learning goal that they have identified themselves or that we, as teachers, have set.

Metacognitive learners recognise what they find easy or difficult. They understand the demands of a particular learning task and are able to identify different approaches they could use to tackle a problem. Metacognitive learners are also able to make adjustments to their learning as they monitor their progress towards a particular learning goal.

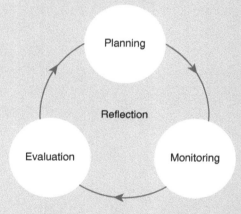

Figure 8.1: A helpful way to think about the phases involved in metacognition.

During the *planning* phase, students think about the explicit learning goal we have set and what we are asking them to do. As teachers, we need to make clear to students what success looks like in any given task before they embark on it. Students build on their prior knowledge, reflect on strategies they have used before and consider how they will approach the new task.

As students put their plan into action, they are constantly *monitoring* the progress they are making towards their learning goal. If the strategies they had decided to use are not working, they may decide to try something different.

Once they have completed the task, students determine how successful the strategy they used was in helping them to achieve their learning goal. During this *evaluation* phase, students think about what went well and what didn't go as well to help them decide what they could do differently next time. They may also think about what other types of problems they could solve using the same strategy.

Reflection is a fundamental part of the plan–monitor–evaluate process and there are various ways in which we can support our students to reflect on their learning process. In order to apply a metacognitive approach, students need access to a set of strategies that they can use and a classroom environment that encourages them to explore and develop their metacognitive skills.

Why teach metacognitive skills?

Research evidence suggests that the use of metacognitive skills plays an important role in successful learning. Metacognitive practices help students to monitor their own progress and take control of their learning. Metacognitive learners think about and learn from their mistakes and modify their learning strategies accordingly. Students who use metacognitive techniques find it improves their academic achievement across subjects, as it helps them transfer what they have learnt from one context to another context, or from a previous task to a new task.

What are the challenges of developing students' metacognitive skills?

For metacognition to be commonplace in the classroom, we need to encourage students to take time to think about and learn from their mistakes. Many students are afraid to make mistakes, meaning that they are less likely to take risks, explore new ways of thinking or tackle unfamiliar problems. We as teachers are instrumental in shaping the culture of learning in a classroom. For metacognitive practices to thrive, students need to feel confident enough to make mistakes, to discuss their mistakes and ultimately to view them as valuable, and often necessary, learning opportunities.

Thinking about thinking

'Metacognition' is a concept that may seem sophisticated and complicated. It isn't. It means something fairly simple. It means *thinking about thinking*, or *knowing about knowing*. It's about the difference between various thinking processes that result in knowledge and understanding. Thinking is not a reflex like swallowing, coughing or blinking. It is a *process*, and like all processes, it has organising principles and procedural stages.

Students tend to be preoccupied with *what* they need to learn. Teachers need to help them to understand *how* they need to learn. Some of this understanding of how to learn will be common to all students; for example, all students will need to retain some knowledge in their memory. However, some of this understanding will be specific to individuals; for example, some students will need to reinforce learning by repetition, while others will need to reinforce learning by talking about it, or through practical activity. Still others will need to reinforce learning by making notes or by representing knowledge graphically.

Some students learn best by listening, some by writing and others by drawing or by doing. Students need to know their learning strengths and weaknesses, and teachers need to adapt their teaching to the preferred or most effective **individual learning style** of students.

Organising principles of a thinking and learning process

Students will be helped as metacognitive learners if they see that learning can be organised into these main categories:

- Subject-specific content – mainly factual knowledge (e.g. plot and character in a novel)
- subject-specific assessment modes and criteria
- subject-specific skills and terminology (e.g. metaphor, allusion, narrative perspective)
- generic skills used and useful in other subjects (e.g. interpretation, analysis, comparison and contrast)
- generic skills of information-seeking, self-testing and dialogue with teacher and other students.

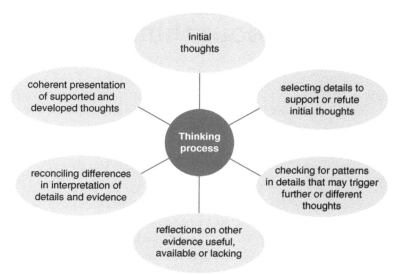

Figure 8.2: Procedural stages in a thinking and learning activity.

Clearer understanding

In other words, thinking is a *discipline*, not a spontaneous burst of opinion or feeling. The result of thinking – or the intention of thinking – is *clearer understanding*. In terms of metacognition, understanding itself has layers and distinctions.

Teacher Tip

Students need to recognise different kinds of **understanding**. Ask them to discuss the difference between:

- *'I understand the instructions for assembling a table-tennis table.'*
- *'I understand why you don't want me to stay overnight with my friends the weekend before exams.'*
- *'I understand the second law of thermodynamics.'*

a) is about understanding a mechanical procedure; b) is about understanding another person's values and perspectives; c) is about understanding a concept.

Understanding facts

Take the word 'understanding', for example. There are simple and more complex levels of understanding. We may understand a statement because it provides all the explicit information we need. For example:

- *'It's Tuesday.'* – This is a fact concerning time. It makes clear that the day concerned is not Wednesday or Saturday. It's about *When*.
- *'It's cold.'* or *'I'm cold.'* – These are facts concerning temperature and personal comfort. They are about *What*.
- *'She lives on the Roundway Park.'* – This is a fact about location. It makes clear that someone does not live elsewhere (e.g. Airport Drive Apartments). It's about *Where*.

There are other aspects of understanding. These involve more than extracted information and require some *processing* of the information.

Understanding the limitations of facts

This is where the fact alone raises some further thinking, usually in the form of a question seeking more information provided than in the fact:

- Could there be something special about Tuesday or not?
- Is the air conditioning properly adjusted?
- May that address be significant?

Understanding the implications of facts

This is where the fact takes on more significance when connected to some other knowledge and understanding, because of a wider context of reference. For example, the implications for the above bullet points could be:

- Tuesday is the only day when the 10.00 train doesn't run.
- If you're cold when it's 24 degrees, you may have something wrong with you.
- So, she can afford to live in the new development where apartments cost enough to keep ordinary people out.

Teacher Tip

Students need to be able to recognise implied meaning.

Ask them what is being implied here:

a *'With respect, I completely support your right to a strong opinion and am sure you have thought carefully about all the arguments for and against.'*

b *'I'm not someone who ever asks for help when I'm in difficulty, so I'll just have to walk home in the dark now I've lost my wallet and don't have enough money for a taxi.'*

The implication of a) is that the speaker disagrees with the other but is being very careful to create no offence or seem too assertive.

The implication of b) is that the speaker hopes that help will be offered without having to ask for it directly.

In Literature, reading to understand facts is a very small part of the study focus. In literary reading, understanding needs to embrace ideas, feelings and attitudes.

Cognitive skills

As we have seen in earlier chapters, understanding by extracting information from a text is a basic skill. There are other skills that require more active reading and responding to a text. These are information-processing skills. They require different thinking (cognitive) processes.

Four essential cognitive skills

1 Translation. Sometimes the cognitive activity is *translating* meaning to another reader, such as when we explain or interpret meaning.

2 Speculation. Sometimes the cognitive activity is *speculating* about a text, such as when we reflect upon meaning or explore possibilities of meaning. Guessing, predicting and theorising are familiar kinds of speculation.

3 **Application.** Sometimes the cognitive activity is *applying* the text to other things, finding interest and significance by connecting it or comparing it to other events, situations or texts.

4 **Investigation.** Sometimes the cognitive activity is *investigative*, such as when we approach a text analytically in order to evaluate it.

These four different information–processing skills for reading involve a range of cognitive processes that can be developed and linked to the assessment objectives of the Literature syllabus. These cognitive skills can all be linked to the four components of the 'world of Literature' study.

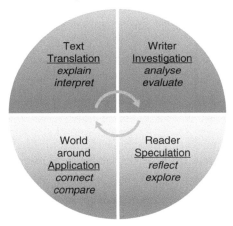

Figure 8.3: Cognitive skills for reading.

▣ LESSON IDEA ONLINE 8.1: DEVELOPING SKILLS: FROM UNDERSTANDING TO RESPONSE

The focus of this lesson idea is on explained comment that refers to a specific detail and a specific kind of response to what students have read.

Understanding and response

Understanding does not happen on its own. It is usually a bigger or a smaller part of a larger response. Our general response to things, including how we *understand* things, is not just a matter of intelligence.

Approaches to learning and teaching Literature in English

Other things affect our response and understanding. If someone shouts at us we may *understand* why they are shouting but the understanding will be less than a *response* of fear, annoyance or anger. If we read something when we are in a happy, sad or impatient mood, our mood will have an effect on our response and understanding. There may be aspects of our culture that affect the way we respond to literature, just as they may affect our response to life.

Response to literature is more than knowledge about a text. Knowledge about the plot and the characters is obviously important as original material for a response, but the response is made up of other personal ingredients. Response to literature includes the way that it makes us feel, and how our ideas and attitudes may be affected by what we read. It's also about how our feelings, ideas and attitudes may make us respond negatively to texts.

Teacher Tip

Students need to know how to turn understanding into response. Ask them to discuss/write about the difference between these pairs of statements:

a *This novel is about the way people survived when their car broke down in the desert.*
b *I found it sad when I got to the part where they had to walk across the desert to survive.*

a) describes the novel content; b) describes the reader's reaction to the novel content.

a *Shakespeare's sonnet suggests that true love doesn't change when people change.*
b *Most people would find it hard to accept that love doesn't change when people change.*

b) comments on the impact of Shakespeare's idea on people in general.

It's not just our mood that affects our response. Sometimes we react to an event or a person (or read a text) with a response and understanding that comes from our age, gender or culture. So it's always worth checking out how far our response and understanding are affected by these things and the world around us. What we perceive is not always down to what is in front of us.

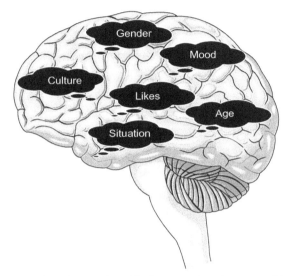

Figure 8.4: Know what's in your head before your head starts making judgements.

Reading and rereading

It's a good idea to prompt students to compare a first reading to a second reading. What they notice on rereading may be different from their first reading – and this may affect their understanding. It may also affect their interpretation. Generally speaking, we all need to check out our reactions to something to know if we have seen the whole picture.

A first and second glance at Figure 8.5 will make the point. It will also make the point that two people may see the same thing differently – and that's an important lesson in understanding the effect of visual images, literary texts or events in life.

Figure 8.5: Two people may see the same thing differently. What do you see here?

Teacher Tip

Remind your students that ambiguity is not a problem. It can mean that:

- there are two or more intended (or unintended) meanings in a text
- there are two or more ways of interpreting a text.

☑ LESSON IDEA ONLINE 8.2: DEVELOPING SKILLS: WRITER-MANIPULATED RESPONSES IN POETRY

This lesson idea shows how a poem's structure rather than its language is part of a writer's manipulation of conflicting sympathies in a text.

☑ LESSON IDEA ONLINE 8.3: DEVELOPING SKILLS: APPRECIATING THE FUNCTIONS OF NARRATIVE

This lesson idea prompts students to see how narrative details can be purposefully used to create a sense of menace and tension about what is to happen.

**☑ LESSON IDEA ONLINE 8.4: DEVELOPING SKILLS –
APPRECIATING CHARACTERISATION IN DRAMA**

This lesson idea prompts students to develop their understanding
of genre through reference to performance cues, characterisation,
structure and audience appeal.

Consider other people's perspectives, too, and you will understand how
the same facts produce different interpretations. In Literature study,
different readers may have different interpretations of what they have
read. Your students should be aware that two people looking at the same
text will notice different things, value different things and understand
different things. This is not a problem; it is a source of interesting
material that gets your students to reflect, to compare and to evaluate.

Summary

In this chapter you have explored some of the practicalities of
metacognition by considering various kinds of understanding. You
have considered:

- how to structure a thinking and learning sequence

- how to organise learning by subject-specific and generic
  principles

- how specific categories of applied understanding are linked to
  the central model of Literature skills

- the importance of helping students to know how they know
  what they know.

9 | Language awareness

What is language awareness?

For many students, English is an additional language. It might be their second or perhaps their third language. Depending on the school context, students might be learning all or just some of their subjects through English.

For all students, regardless of whether they are learning through their first language or an additional language, language is a vehicle for learning. It is through language that students access the learning intentions of the lesson and communicate their ideas. It is our responsibility as teachers to ensure that language doesn't present a barrier to learning.

One way to achieve this is to support our colleagues in becoming more language-aware. Language awareness is sensitivity to, and an understanding of, the language demands of our subject and the role these demands play in learning. A language-aware teacher plans strategies and scaffolds the appropriate support to help students overcome these language demands.

Why is it important for teachers of other subjects to be language-aware?

Many teachers are surprised when they receive a piece of written work that suggests a student who has no difficulties in everyday communication has had problems understanding the lesson. Issues arise when teachers assume that students who have attained a high degree of fluency and accuracy in everyday social English therefore have a corresponding level of academic language proficiency. Whether English is a student's first language or an additional language, students need time and the appropriate support to become proficient in academic language. This is the language that they are mostly exposed to in school and will be required to reproduce themselves. It will also scaffold their ability to access higher order thinking skills and improve levels of attainment.

What are the challenges of language awareness?

Many teachers of non-language subjects worry that there is no time to factor language support into their lessons, or that language is something they know little about. Some teachers may think that language support is not their role. However, we need to work with these teachers to create inclusive classrooms where all students can access the curriculum and where barriers to learning are reduced as much as possible. An increased awareness of the language needs of students aims to reduce any obstacles that learning through an additional language might present.

This doesn't mean that all teachers need to know the names of grammatical structures or need to be able to use the appropriate linguistic labels. What it does mean is that we all need to understand the challenges our students face, including their language level, and plan some strategies to help them overcome these challenges. These strategies do not need to take a lot of additional time and should eventually become integral to our process of planning, teaching and reflecting on our practice. We may need to support other teachers so that they are clear about the vocabulary and language that is specific to their subject, and how to teach, reinforce and develop it.

Familiarity of language and literature

All of your students' work in English Literature will involve a specific language awareness in their reading, and in their writing about their reading. Their reading will involve them with writers who use language very skilfully. If your students have a limited grasp of the English language, this will present them with various difficulties. For example, they may find difficulty with a writer's grammar, vocabulary or idiomatic expressions. They may also find difficulties in understanding references to places, events, customs and cultures. This will be even more obvious when they are studying literature from previous centuries. You can help them through these difficulties by providing explanations for vocabulary, explaining references and adapting grammatical features into more familiar forms.

Your own language awareness will be important here. When you sense that your students are struggling with vocabulary, you need to provide alternatives in English or in the students' native language. You also need to make them aware that some English words have different meanings in different specialist subject use. For example, some words have very specific meanings when used in science:

- **Work**. A force acting upon an object to cause a displacement.
- **Force**. That which changes or tends to change the state of rest.
- **Resistance**. Anything in a circuit that slows down the flow of electrical current.
- **Power**. The rate at which work is done.
- **Field**. An assignment of a quantity to every point in space.

In international schools, students will have varying degrees of familiarity and confidence in English. They will be helped if you make links between their English Language study and their study of English Literature. However, there will be additional linguistic demands specific to the study of Literature and to writing about Literature.

Apart from issues of language familiarity, there are issues that are specific to Literature examinations. Your students need to know what is meant by common terms used in examination questions. They also need to know about forms of language appropriate to writing about literature in an examination. This chapter will help you to help them with all of these issues.

The language of texts

The most obvious characteristics of a literary text can be seen in the first few sentences or lines.

Narrative voice

In novels, the most obvious differences between texts is in the narrative voice. This means the voice of the story-teller. A writer may choose a first-person narrative style because it makes the story realistic by being told by a character as if it is an autobiography. For example:

> If you've decided you're gonna read this book, I'm gonna be dead honest with you. I'm not the sort of guy you normally find writing a book. In fact, I'm surprised I've written it at all, but I had some help from a friend of mine who's a teacher, and he said I've got a story to tell that people would like to read.

A writer may choose a third-person narrative style because it makes the characters realistic by being told by someone recording events that seem to have been real events occuring in the past. For example:

> Satish emailed me a year ago, several years after he had left school. He had done some travelling, and tried various jobs, including telesales in Kolkata, palm-oil production in Malaysia and cooking for tourists on a dhow in Dubai Creek. He said these experiences had given him plenty of ideas about work and communication in the globalised world of the twenty-first century. He wanted to know how to make something of his experience. When I told him he should write it all down, he said he hated writing. Then he asked if I would help.

⊡ LESSON IDEA ONLINE 9.1: THE LANGUAGE OF EXAM QUESTIONS

This lesson idea gives students practice in identifying common question types in Literature assessment, with a focus on key command words. It illustrates a wide range of questions, covering prose, poetry and drama.

Tense

The second most obvious difference between texts is their use of tense. A writer may choose a **present-tense narrative style** because it makes the story's events seem to happen in real time. It gives a sense of immediacy and makes the reader see the story from the character's point of view. For example:

> It's late at night and I'm writing this before I go to bed because otherwise I'll forget what I want to say. I'm giving myself three months between jobs to see if I can write something that makes sense to me and others. I've taken a bit of advice from my old English teacher and I've told my lovely partner that if this doesn't work I'll go back to earning some money.

A writer may choose a **past-tense narrative style** because it makes it seem as if the writer is recording events that actually took place. It gives it a sense of authenticity and makes the reader see the story from the author's point of view. For example:

> The boy and the girl stood still and silently gazed upon the sight before them. The remains of their tents were scattered all around after the storm, and the poles were sticking out at odd angles. All around were clothes and camping equipment that the wind had scattered and the rain had soaked.

Teacher Tip

Use your students' knowledge of English to reinforce their awareness of literary matters. Ask them to:

- write an account of an event in the first person, then in the third person
- write an account of the same event in the present tense, then in the past tense.

LESSON IDEA 9.2: CHANGING THE TENSE

Take one of the examples of prose using different tenses. Change the tense of the passage, for example from past to present or present to past.

75

LESSON IDEA 9.3: CHANGING THE NARRATIVE VOICE

Take one of the examples of prose using different narrative voices. Change the narrative voice, for example, from first person to third person or third person to first person.

⊡ LESSON IDEA ONLINE 9.4: THE LANGUAGE OF CRITICAL RESPONSE

This lesson idea prompts students to see the limitations of response which is based on 'story' ingredients, and shows the difference between a narrative response, a descriptive response and a critical response.

Style

The third most obvious difference between texts is in the kind of English used. A writer may choose a **Standard English style** because he/she wants to appeal to a wide audience of educated English speakers. For example:

'Nothing's Changed', by Tatumkula Africa

Small round hard stones click
under my heels,
seeding grasses thrust
bearded seeds
into trouser cuffs, cans,
trodden on, crunch
in tall, purple-flowering,
amiable weeds.

Writers may choose a **dialect style** because they want to appeal to a particular community or realistically portray a particular community – or because they feel pride in the special nature of their dialect. For example:

'Checking out me history', by John Agard

Dem tell me
Dem tell me
Wha dem want to tell me

Bandage up me eye with me own history
  Blind me to me own identity

Dem tell me bout 1066 and all dat
Dem tell me bout Dick Whittington and he cat
But Toussaint L'Ouverture
  No dem never tell me bout dat

Teacher Tip

In an international school there will be rich resources of language variety. Ask students to find and present to the class some examples of dialect in a specific language.

Some texts are written in a language that may seem strange to readers today. This has resulted in various attempts to rewrite them in a simple form of modern English. Compare the following two texts, where Hamlet's famous soliloquy has been rewritten for a modern audience.

Ask students to discuss/write about:

a how the modern version makes the text clearer for you
b anything that has been lost by rewriting it this way.

To be, or not to be, that is the question – *Whether 'tis nobler in the mind to suffer* *The slings and arrows of outrageous fortune* *Or to take arms against a sea of troubles,* *And by opposing end them.* *To die, to sleep,–* *No more; and by a sleep to say we end* *The heart-ache, and the thousand natural shocks* *That flesh is heir to – 'tis a consummation* *Devoutly to be wished.*	The question is: is it better to be alive or dead? Is it nobler to put up with all the nasty things that luck throws your way, or to fight against all those troubles by simply putting an end to them once and for all? Dying, sleeping – that's all dying is – a sleep that ends all the heartache and shocks that life on earth gives us – that's an achievement to wish for.

The language of examinations

When your students are faced with an examination paper, they need to know what kind of response is required, as indicated the wording of the questions.

There are two aspects of the language of examinations:

- The language of questioning, where specific kinds of response are prompted by key command words.
- The language of assessment, where specific levels of response skills are indicated by key words acting as rungs in the ladder of performance.

Exam questions: key command words

- 'What' questions usually require an answer based on knowledge of character or events.
- 'How' questions usually require an answer based on understanding of the writer's craft – mainly related to form, structure and language.

Versions of these command words are:

- 'How far' – these questions usually require a kind of debating response, measuring the accuracy/relevance of various interpretations or opinions.
- 'In what ways' – these questions require an answer based on the writer's craft and technique, mainly related to form, structure and language.

Other key commands are:

- 'Explain' – give an account with accurate knowledge and understanding.
- 'Explore' – try out a number of possible explanations of knowledge and understanding.
- 'Analyse' – investigate and classify a range of details to find a pattern or a significant inconsistency.

The language of Literature study

Other terms students need to be familiar with are:

- character – a person created for a fictional purpose
- **characterisation** – the art and craft of making fictional characters believable
- **persona** – the character created by a writer (usually in poetry) as the speaker in a literary work
- methods – techniques
- effects – kinds of emotional or intellectual impact on the reader
- form – the literary genre (e.g. sonnet, first person narrative, monologues)
- structure – the internal shape of a text and relationship between its parts
- **imagery** – simile, metaphor and personification
- **rhetorical devices** - rhetorical question, repetition (for a specific effect), hyperbole, irony
- presents – brings to the reader's notice: can be a focus on how something is presented or the author's attitude and purpose in presenting something
- ideas – thoughts
- feelings – emotions
- attitudes – conscious or unconscious typical responses and postures
- relationships – status and co-existence of pairs and groups, and interaction
- setting – the time and/or place chosen by the writer
- dramatic terms – act, scene, dialogue, stage direction, audience, soliloquy, characterisation, dramatic irony
- poetic terms – rhyme, rhythm, stanza, couplet, blank verse, free verse, sonnet, tone, mood, persona, monologue
- prose terms – chapter, paragraph, sentence, clause, phrase, dialogue, narrator, viewpoint, characterisation.

Teacher Tip

Collect a range of practice questions so that your students are familiar with key command words and their implications for the kind of answer required.

The language of assessment: key terms for levels of response

Lower-level attainment

- An **explained response** is one that shows competent understanding of the question and the text.
- A **supported response** is one that illustrates competent understanding of the question and the text with relevant quotation.
- A **descriptive response** is one that provides details of character, plot or setting but does not relate to authorial purpose, authorial craft or effects on readers.

For example, stating that Lady Macbeth is manipulative and provocative is an explained response. With a relevant quotation, it would be a supported response. With a narrative account of how she behaves it would be a descriptive response.

Higher-level attainment

- A **sophisticated response** shows a combination of informed and independent subtlety and complexity.
- A **perceptive response** shows independent discovery and comment, making subtle or forceful use of a detail that others would not find significant, or seeing the implications or applications of an idea beyond the immediate fictional context.
- An **insightful response** is the ability to see more than what is immediately visible and already explicit in print. Insightful reading finds significance in the implicit.

☑ LESSON IDEA ONLINE 9.5: THE LANGUAGE OF SPOKEN VERSE

This lesson idea prompts students to analyse the way sound is exploited as a literary study. The sound manipulation in the poem 'Lament for steam' is evident in the exploitation of vowel sounds and consonantal sounds.

The language of writing about texts

Your students are likely to be assessed on the way that they write about their Literature study, so their expression is important, as is fluent and accurate English. For example the assessment objectives from the Cambridge IGCSE English Literature syllabus provide the following guidance:

AO4: Use a range of vocabulary and sentence structures for clarity, purpose and effect, with accurate spelling and punctuation.

In addition, you need to pay attention to use of English for specific Literature study purposes. This means that second-language English speakers need practice in developing a style of writing specific to Literature exams. A typical assessment objective might be:

AO1: Students should be able to:

- **maintain** a critical style and develop an informed personal response
- **use** textual references, including quotations, to support and illustrate interpretations.

AO2: Analyse the language, form and structure used by a writer to create meanings and effects, **using relevant subject terminology where appropriate**.

Maintaining a critical style

A critical style expresses informed comment on aspects of genre, authorial craft and purpose. It is based on analytical examination of textual detail and evaluates the writer's achievement in appealing to and influencing readers. A critical style is one that avoids narrative retelling of the story and avoids a descriptive account of plot and characters.

Writing about interpretation

An explained meaning is usually presented as a factual statement. *Interpretations* are not facts – they are ways of making sense of facts. So, writing that 'This means …' asserts what is a fact. Writing 'This could mean ...', 'This may mean ...' shows awareness of alternatives, tentatively expressing what may be true, but may be personal, partly true or possibly true. The easiest way for a student to introduce an interpretation is by reference to themselves or to other readers. For example:

- 'Some readers would see this as ...'
- 'I think this shows ...'
- 'There are several ways of looking at this ...'

Writing about characters and characterisation

It is easy to fall into a trap of writing about characters as if they are real, and very easy when a writer has made the characters seem very realistic. Students need to remember that the focus in Literature study is on the writer's craft – the ways in which he or she makes characters so believable that they could be real. So, students need to avoid statements that treat the characters as if they are real people. For example:

- 'Mr Birling thinks that ...'
- 'Romeo speaks in rhyming couplets ...'
- 'Jack becomes more like a savage when he starts using face paints.'

Instead, they need to focus on the author's craft in making the characters think, talk and behave the way they do. The easiest way to do this is to include the writer as the person behind the character. For example:

- 'Priestley makes the audience see that Birling thinks ...'
- 'Shakespeare writes Romeo's lines in rhyming couplets here because ...'
- 'Golding shows Jack's increasing savagery by showing him using face paints.'

☑ LESSON IDEA ONLINE 9.6: CONNECTING VERBAL IMAGERY WITH VISUAL IMAGERY

This lesson idea looks at the poem 'Portrait of a Machine', by Louis Untermeyer, and prompts students to think about alternative words that would make sense in the context, before seeing the words chosen by the writer. It then prompts them to connect verbal imagery with visual imagery.

Using textual references, including quotations, to support and illustrate interpretations

Quotations are the evidence that supports a comment on any aspect of a writer's work. Quotations can be very short or several lines long.

Short quotations are best integrated into the comment. For example:

'By using words like "beggars", "coughed" and "hags" Owen creates a scene of pain and misery to contrast with the idea that war is something fine and glorious.'

Longer quotations should be followed by investigation of several parts of the quotation. For example:

'"Stuttering rifles' rapid rattle". In this line Owen deliberately uses short-vowelled words to create a sense of rapid movement, and also uses the consonants "t" in "stuttering" and "rattle" and "r" "rifle", "rapid" and "rattle" to reproduce a sound like that of gunfire. The alliteration helps him to convey a sense of urgency and violence as part of his attempt to show the reality rather than the propaganda fiction of war.'

Using relevant subject terminology where appropriate

Students need to know the technical vocabulary of Literature study, but they do not need to make this knowledge the main part of their answer. The key terms here are 'relevant' and 'where appropriate'. Mechanical identification of features from a list is a very basic part of a literary reading response. It shows some understanding, but what matters is explaining and exploring the purpose and effect of the identified features. More important is a genuine personal response to meanings and how they are conveyed. The five essentials are:

- ideas, attitudes and feelings
- language – for example vocabulary, verbs, nouns, adjectives and adverbs, and grammatical features such as sentence structures
- style – for example irony, **pathos**, realism, symbolism, narrative, dialogue, alliteration, assonance, rhythm, rhyme, metaphor, simile
- purpose – authorial ideas and purposes
- effect – impacts on readers.

Teacher Tip

All of these aspects of writing about Literature need practice. Try writing examples of inappropriate comments for your students to turn into comments that match the descriptions in this chapter. Here are some examples of inappropriate comments:

- The writer makes you feel you are there.
- The writer's details of setting include sights and smells as well as time and weather to help the reader to imagine the place as a real place.
- The writer uses lots of words that make you feel strong emotions about X.
- The writer uses words such as 'cruel', 'deliberate' and 'spiteful' to make the reader feel an emotion of dislike for X.
- The writer uses lots of imagery to bring out what the character is like.
- The writer uses similes such as 'like a bear' and 'hawk-like', and the metaphor 'flew along the road' to make the man seem powerful and quick in movement.

The spirit of the Cambridge IGCSE English Literature syllabus is that students develop the confidence to respond directly and personally to their reading. Questions are designed to prompt students to think for themselves rather than to remember and reuse prepared responses, and confident students can express individual views of their reading based on their own choice of textual details rather than relying on secondary reading in study aids.

Summary

In this chapter you have looked at the ways in which specific language awareness is required for reading literary texts. You have considered:

- the different characteristics of the language of text
- how to understand different types of questions and the way they prompt specific kinds of response
- how to write with appropriate style about Literature.

Inclusive education

What is inclusive education?

Individual differences among students will always exist; our challenge as teachers is to see these not as problems to be fixed but as opportunities to enrich and make learning accessible for all. Inclusion is an effort to make sure all students receive whatever specially designed instruction and support they need to succeed as learners.

An inclusive teacher welcomes all students and finds ways to accept and accommodate each individual student. An inclusive teacher identifies existing barriers that limit access to learning, then finds solutions and strategies to remove or reduce those barriers. Some barriers to inclusion are visible; others are hidden or difficult to recognise.

Barriers to inclusion might be the lack of educational resources available for teachers or an inflexible curriculum that does not take into account the learning differences that exist among all learners, across all ages. We also need to encourage students to understand each others' barriers, or this itself may become a barrier to learning.

Students may experience challenges because of any one or a combination of the following:

- behavioural and social skill difficulties
- communication or language disabilities
- concentration difficulties
- conflict in the home or that caused by political situations or national emergency
- executive functions, such as difficulties in understanding, planning and organising
- hearing impairments, acquired congenitally or through illness or injury
- literacy and language difficulties
- numeracy difficulties
- physical or neurological impairments, which may or may not be visible
- visual impairments, ranging from mild to severe.

We should be careful, however, not to label a student and create further barriers in so doing, particularly if we ourselves are not qualified to make a diagnosis. Each student is unique but it is our management of their learning environment that will decide the extent of the barrier and the need for it to be a factor. We need to be aware of a student's readiness to learn and their readiness for school.

Why is inclusive education important?

Teachers need to find ways to welcome all students and organise their teaching so that each student gets a learning experience that makes engagement and success possible. We should create a good match between what we teach and how we teach it, and what the student needs and is capable of. We need not only to ensure access but also make sure each student receives the support and individual attention that result in meaningful learning.

What are the challenges of an inclusive classroom?

Some students may have unexpected barriers. Those who consistently do well in class may not perform in exams, or those who are strong at writing may be weaker when speaking. Those who are considered to be the brightest students may also have barriers to learning. Some students may be working extra hard to compensate for barriers they prefer to keep hidden; some students may suddenly reveal limitations in their ability to learn, using the techniques they have been taught. We need to be aware of all corners of our classroom, be open and put ourselves in our students' shoes.

Creating an inclusive learning classroom

Inclusive education means education that caters for all students, irrespective of individual differences. And any class on the planet will contain individual differences. Students may wear school uniform and they may share many uniform characteristics, but there will be at least as many differences in their personalities as there are similarities. These differences have an impact on their learning – and on your teaching. Creating an **inclusive learning** classroom means catering for more than students' physical and intellectual ability: it means catering for a range of capacities, personalities, motivations and attitudes. *It also means helping students to see that their personal experiences and cultures can be included in a response to Literature.*

The main learning-related differences

These are easily observed and generally catered for. Here are some of the main learning-related differences that you can expect to find in most classes:

- **Physical**. Some students may have visual, aural or fine motor limitations that impact on their learning. You would expect the school and all its teachers to be aware of this and to have strategies in place to support such students. For instance, some students may need a learning support assistant, or large-print texts, or to be seated near the front, while others may need visual/auditory pre-distributed learning support materials.
- **Intelligence**. Some students may have mental speed and agility when encountering and managing complex, subtle or abstract concepts. Some students, for example, may not understand abstract definitions, but may be helped by being given concrete examples.
- **Motivation**. Some students may have little interest or experience in reading for pleasure, or reading literature. They may need video or graphical versions, or small samples of engaging and appealing texts.

There are other capacities that affect learning, and may or may not be related to physical ability or intelligence:

- **Memory**. Some students may be eager, committed and ambitious, but poor in memory recall.

- **Language**. Some students may lack the English competence needed to cope with tasks and texts in English Literature.
- **Learning style**. Some students may be primarily aural, oral, practical, literary or kinaesthetic in their learning style. Teachers know those students who can talk better than – or more than – they can write.

There are also motivational factors that are internal:

- **Ambition**. Some students may be driven by ambition to be, for example, lawyers, doctors or financiers, which can sustain them even in subjects they do not like or intend to pursue further.
- **Commitment**. Some students may be weak or strong in energy, interest, concentration and persistence.
- **Receptivity**. Some students are more ready, able and willing to receive instruction and guidance than others.
- **Emotion**. Some students may have a need for reassurance or approval, or be afraid of seeming slow or confused.

There are other motivational factors that are external:

- **Culture.** Some students may be culturally determined by their home or community influences to favour or resist certain kinds of learning and certain kinds of learning content.
- **Gender.** Some students may be influenced by gender stereotypes and expectations that impact on their learning.
- **Family.** Some students may be under strong (sometimes excessive) pressure to succeed because their parents are themselves successful and ambitious, or their older siblings have been successful.

Teacher Tip

Beware of defining individual students by one particular 'learning style'. All of us, students and teachers, are more complex than that. We are all a mixture of many of these things – and not always the same mixture on a Sunday or a Thursday!

In short, any group of three people will have significant differences as learners. If you have 30 students in your class, you can expect the differences to be more numerous than the similarities. Your teaching will need to take into account the special needs, abilities and preferences of all of them. That's a lot to ask! Some students may not be confident about expressing different opinions: if you show that all opinions are welcomed and valued, they will be willing to offer more of themselves in class discussion – and in writing.

Teacher Tip

On a list of the students in your class, make notes about them individually as learners using the categories of learning-related differences. You may find you have already had these in your head, but you may find that you gain a better grasp of their needs, weaknesses and strengths as learners.

Managing different students

Some schools adopt a policy of setting classes by ability to remove the greatest differences in a group of students. This does help to create a more uniform group, but no setting will ever remove all of the differences between learners. Usually, classes are grouped by ability – either by general academic ability or by English language ability. You can still expect to find significant differences in motivation and responsiveness in a group with a range of limited ability.

Other schools adopt a policy of mixed ability, usually because this avoids the problem of having a bottom set of reluctant students that someone has to teach. A more positive, democratic, reason is that weaker students are not discouraged by seeing themselves as lower-performing members of the group, and have the chance of learning from the behaviour, contributions and attitudes of the more able.

Task differentiation

Whatever class you are teaching, you need to provide for **differences**. You can do this by various means:

- You may give **differentiated** tasks, giving easier tasks to the less able and more demanding ones to the more able. The advantage is that the less able are not discouraged by difficulty. The problem with this is that you may set a ceiling of expectation on those you give the easier tasks to.

- You may give the same tasks to all students, but provide differentiated questions to cater for their different abilities. The advantage is that all students feel equally involved in the same task. Again, the problem with this is that weaker students may not be helpfully stretched by tackling more difficult questions.
- You may provide a list of tasks in a sequence of increasing difficulty and challenge. The advantage of this is that all students feel equally involved, but the less able can stop when they feel they can do no more. The problem with this is that laziness rather than ability may influence their persistence.
- You may differentiate by outcome. You would do this by setting the same task and questions for all and assessing what they do. The advantage of this is that it gives students a sense of equality. The problem is that it does not provide differentiated support to take students beyond their existing limits.

Teacher Tip

You can organise your approach to providing **explicit differentiation** or **embedded differentiation** as follows:

- Explicit differentiation can be organised by different coloured worksheets for different abilities.
- Embedded differentiation can be organised by common worksheets with questions sequenced by increasing challenge indicated by the mark tariff.

Differentiated tasks and differentiated questions

Various studies of classroom practice have recorded an extraordinarily high percentage of teachers' questions, such as "Are you on page 23?" or "Have you been listening?" as merely procedural and managerial. A **professionalised approach** to teacher questioning is driven by a focus on the content and cognitive aspects of learning. A **personalised approach** to teacher questioning is driven by awareness of students' differences as learners. What you need is a questioning repertoire based on differentiated challenge for a range of ability in one class. This has been supported for many years by building on the cognitive taxonomy model created by Benjamin Bloom.

Bloom's cognitive taxonomy model

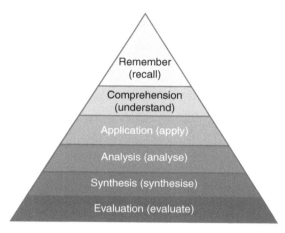

Figure 10.1: Bloom's cognitive taxonomy model.

Lower-order questioning

- **Recall questions** – does the student *remember*?
- **Comprehension questions** – does the student *understand*?

Higher-order questioning

- **Application questions** – can the student *apply* a rule or a technique in a new context?
- **Analysis questions** – can the student identify causes and connections, and give examples to support?
- **Synthesis questions** – can the student make predictions and solve problems by linking ideas?
- **Evaluation questions** – can the student judge the quality of ideas and explanations, and prioritise and reconcile conflicts?

This model of cognitive differentiation and progression gives a strong basis for targeting individuals and targeting levels of skill. Here is an example of a teacher's repertoire based on Bloom's cognitive taxonomy model:

1 **Recall**
   - Tell me what happened.
   - What happened after…
   - Who knows why/where/when etc.

2 **Understand**
   - What were the reasons for…
   - What does X mean when she says…
   - Why was X feeling so…

3 **Apply**
   - Does this remind you of anything else you've read?
   - Where else could you find…
   - What has been happening in the news recently that is similar to…

4 **Analyse**
   - Is it *always* true that…
   - Would you *sometimes* agree that…When would you not agree that…
   - Are you *certain* that…

5 **Synthesise**
   - Why does X say this on page 34 and this on page 98…
   - What do you find similar in Chapter 2 and Chapter 19…
   - What can you find to suggest that X has/has not changed over…

6 **Evaluate**
   - Do you feel sad/happy when…
   - What would you do if…
   - Would you do the same as…

Teacher Tip

Cognitive ability is not everything… Bloom's model is useful, but remember that he was a cognitive psychologist, not an English teacher. He certainly wasn't a teacher of English Literature. His taxonomy is restricted to cognitive features, whereas response to Literature involves far more human resources than the cognitive. Dealing with texts rich in values, feelings, ideas, attitudes engages different parts of a student's personality. If Literature is important for anything it is because it promotes the affective as well as the cognitive. Feelings matter!

De Bono's cognitive-affective model

Edward De Bono offers a better model of response. His model is much more suited to learning in Literature and to individuals in the English classroom. This is partly because he treats his categories horizontally rather than vertically, and partly because he doesn't limit human responses only to the cognitive. He presented his model of response in the form of classroom activity in which students were given different hats to wear, each hat representing a different mode of valued response.

De Bono's Thinking Hats		
The White Hat	**The Red Hat**	**The Black Hat**
The neutral one: facts, figures, numbers.	The emotional one: feelings, hunches, instincts, personal views.	The judgemental one: the judge, critical, looks for negatives.
The Yellow Hat	**The Green Hat**	**The Blue Hat**
The little ray of sunshine: looks for positives, benefits and always sees the good.	The creative one: creative thinking, new possibilities and ideas.	The cool one: cool, calm and collected, overview, control of steps, the organiser.

Table 10.1: De Bono's Thinking Hats.

De Bono's work is more useful than Bloom's in the English Literature classroom because it gives equal value to responses that are not merely cerebral or intellectual. It is more differentiated and more democratic. It prompts and values affective as well as cognitive response. As a model of educational differentiation it accepts that there are different intelligences, rather than one brain-specific intelligence. It helps teachers to see the limitation of the question, *'How intelligent is this student?'* It helps you to value and relate to different students by posing the alternative question, *'How is this student intelligent?'*

Teacher Tip

De Bono's cognitive-affective model can be used by giving all students the chance to 'wear the different hats' – which helps diagnosis of strengths and weaknesses. It can also be used to divide the class into groups under the different hats. Another application is to give students who are most successful and at ease with one hat the challenge of 'wearing' another hat that is less to their liking.

Progression

Whether you choose a vertical model of **attainment**, like Bloom's, or a horizontal spread of attainment, like De Bono's, you will need to record progression. This is for your professional needs as you monitor your students' progress, but it is also for your students, because they need to feel approved and successful, and that their work is having an effect.

Recording progress

There are various ways of recording students' progress. Some are public and some personal:

- You may record progress by mapping individual attainment against a version of the syllabus assessment objectives. This could be content- or concept-based.
- You may record progress by mapping attainment against the descriptors of your syllabus mark scheme and attaching to this individual levels or grades.
- You may display progress publicly by recording the term's topics or skills successfully covered on a wall chart where each student sees ticks recording their accomplishments.
- You may prefer to award gold/silver/bronze stars on marked work – and record stars on a wall chart if you want to make a competitive display.

Whatever method you choose, remember that it has two functions. One is a professional function of monitoring learning by **attainment**. The other is of rewarding and motivating individual effort and **achievement**.

Students, classes and the school

Your work in English can be reinforced if your school has a policy for Inclusive Education. There is a need for some cross-curricular common principles and practices so that students can see a coherent educational environment supporting their development.

A common policy could include the following aspects of language and thinking across the curriculum:

- shared language features for common cognitive skills
- distinctive language features of different subjects
- an embedding of common cognitive skills in lesson plans and activities
- common learning sequences.

You may find it useful to go back several centuries to find a questioning model that works on specifics of cognitive skills.

Socratic questioning

Here is another approach to a questioning repertoire which offers a wider range of cognitive responses than the Bloom model. It is very adaptable to the purposes of literary study but does not include some of the dimensions active in the De Bono model. It is known as the Socratic questioning model.

	Response
1: Questions that seek clarification.	
Can you explain that…?	Explaining
What do you mean by…?	Defining
Can you give me an example of…?	Illustrating
How does that help…?	Supporting
2: Questions that probe reasons and evidence.	
Why do you think that…?	Reasoning
How do we know that…?	Justifying
Do you have evidence…?	Referencing
Can you think of another explanation…?	Interpreting

	Response
3. Questions that explore alternative views.	
Can you put it another way…?	Reformulating
Is there another point of view…?	Anticipating
What if someone were to suggest that…?	Conceding
What would someone who disagreed with you say…?	Negotiating
4. Questions that test implications and consequences.	
What follows from what you say…?	Extrapolating
Does that fit with what you said earlier…?	Synthesising
Is it always the case that for that…?	Qualifying
How could you test to see if it were true…?	Validating

Table 10.2: The Socratic questioning model. Adapted from *Teaching Thinking - Philosophical Enquiry in the classroom* by Robert Fisher (1998, Brunel University)

This questioning model can be seen as progressively demanding, or not. Either way, it provides a basis for learning that questions have specific purposes and so require different kinds of responses.

Teacher Tip

Develop an individual student's answering repertoire by asking four questions, one from each category.

Develop students' anticipation of kinds of answers required by asking four questions of a group of four students.

Including cultures and identities

Cross-curricular planning could be initiated by the English department as a support to colleagues in other subjects. This is particularly important in international schools where colleagues with specific subject expertise may not be aware of the role of language in learning. (See Chapter 9 **Language awareness**.)

One of the advantages of an international school is its wealth of cultural diversity. English lessons can draw on language variations and Literature lessons can draw on the range of texts familiar to students. Diversity and commonality can be sources of stimulus and response that make all students feel that involvement in English Literature is enriched by their own experiences.

These lesson ideas each provide stimulus for students to include their own knowledge and experience in their response to texts. The focus on inclusion of personal knowledge and experience draws on memory recall and ability to reflect upon community, culture and family.

☑ LESSON IDEA ONLINE 10.1: WRITER'S EXPERIENCE AND READER'S EXPERIENCE IN POETRY

This lesson idea prompts students to see how texts can also have wider relevance, with equivalents in a range of other cultures.

☑ LESSON IDEA ONLINE 10.2: WRITER'S AND READER'S CULTURE IN PROSE FICTION

This lesson idea prompts students to see how a situation may be culturally specific, and also how it may involve ideas, attitudes and feelings common to all human cultures.

☑ LESSON IDEA ONLINE 10.3: FAMILY RELATIONSHIPS AND CULTURES IN DRAMA

This lesson idea engages students with the relationship between a father and a daughter, and with the ideas, feelings and attitudes which Shakespeare presents so dramatically.

Summary

In this chapter you have looked at different influences on students' learning, and ways in which you can adapt your teaching to their individual learning characteristics. You have considered:

- that the special nature of English Literature study is not limited to the cognitive
- ways in which a professionalised approach to questioning can include all students and support their progression
- ways in which specific learning differences can be supported by practical means
- the importance of a whole-school policy of inclusive education.

Teaching with digital technologies

11

What are digital technologies?

Digital technologies enable our students to access a wealth of up-to-date digital resources, collaborate locally and globally, curate existing material and create new material. They include electronic devices and tools that manage and manipulate information and data.

Why use digital technologies in the classroom?

When used successfully, digital technologies have the potential to transform teaching and learning. The effective use of technology in the classroom encourages active learning, knowledge construction, inquiry and exploration among students. It should enhance an existing task or provide opportunities to do things that could not be done without it. It can also enhance the role of assessment, providing new ways for students to demonstrate evidence of learning.

New technologies are redefining relationships and enabling new opportunities. But there are also risks, so we should encourage our students to be knowledgeable about and responsible in their use of technology. Integrating technology into our teaching helps prepare students for a future rooted in an increasingly digitised world.

What are the challenges of using digital technologies?

The key to ensuring that technology is used effectively is to remember that it is simply a resource, and not an end in itself. As with the use of all resources, the key is not to start with the resource itself, but to start with what you want the student to learn. We need to think carefully about why and how to use technologies as well as evaluating their efficiency and effectiveness.

If students are asked to use digital technologies as part of their homework, it is important that all students are able to access the relevant technology outside school. A school needs to think about a response to any 'digital divide', because if technology is 'adding value', then all students need to be able to benefit. Some schools choose to make resources available to borrow or use in school, or even loan devices to students.

Safety for students and teachers is a key challenge for schools and it is important to consider issues such as the prevention of cyber-bullying, the hacking of personal information, access to illegal or banned materials and distractions from learning. As technology changes, schools and teachers need to adapt and implement policies and rules.

One of the greatest pitfalls is for a teacher to feel that they are not skilled technologists, and therefore not to try. Creative things can be done with simple technology, and a highly effective teacher who knows very little about technology can often achieve much more than a less effective teacher who is a technology expert. Knowing how to use technology is not the same as knowing how to teach with it.

Why use technology?

At this stage in the present century we still have occasion to use pens and paper, but for most young people their main source of information and entertainment is no longer paper-based. Smartphones, tablets and their apps, and social media yield immediate and appealing resources. Online libraries are available from home or classroom, and by smartphone or tablet during the travel between them.

What's positive about this is the free availability of more resources for learning than the world has ever known before. What's not so positive is that some of it is unregulated and of limited worth. Students need to know the difference between online vanity websites and links to commercial websites, and the reputable platforms that may promise less but deliver more. Some online communities may seem appealing and relevant, but may offer more in presentation than in substance.

In terms of studying Literature, a benefit is the wealth of material easily accessed and downloaded. For example, clips from stage and film productions of plays featured in the syllabus, interviews with poets and novelists about their work, and background documentaries on writers, settings, historical periods and social contexts.

A positive aspect in terms of reinforcing study is the scope for forming relationships with other students across the globe and exchanging ideas, materials and experiences. This opens up a community of students larger than the classroom, the school or the country.

This chapter suggests some of the ways digital technology can be used in the classroom or for students' homework, focusing on certain online and digital resources and the application of Microsoft Word as a teaching tool.

Online and digital resources

In this section we look at some of the digital resources available to teachers of Literature.

Project Gutenberg and online texts

Project Gutenberg and other online text repositories are very good resources for selecting passages from texts that can then be used by you or by the students to create various classroom resources for use on paper or on screen, or via memory stick on students' home computers.

You can select a passage from a prose text (novel or short story) that has narrative and dialogue, and copy and paste the extract into a new document. You can then create two texts from it by separating the dialogue and the narrative. This is a good method for drawing attention to the different ways in which narrative and dialogue work. For instance, narrative tends to be Standard English, and *tells* the reader what is necessary, while dialogue tends to be realistic by using dialect and idiom (and *shows* the reader what the character is like). Students can compare the separated texts for what each contributes to a) characterisation b) realism and c) appeal to reader (see Lesson idea 11.2).

Digital sound libraries

Students can draw on their own digital music libraries to find accompaniments suited to public presentations of texts they have studied. Alternatively, they could access sound-effects catalogues to find accompaniments to texts.

Image libraries and movie clips

Students can draw on image banks, clip art, Word art, emojis, etc. to produce a personalised interpretation of a text they have studied. You can create a good classroom or homework resource by **freeze-framing** for a text match. You don't have to be a digital expert to take a still shot from a moving image. You can play a movie clip from a screened version of a text, pause it and do a screen shot by pressing Shift, Command and 3 on a PC, or Shift, Command and 4 on a Mac. You can print out stills, cut them up and get students to match them to selected lines from their text.

Online research

There is a huge wealth of useful material online on places and times that matter in the setting of plays, poems and novels. Similarly, online research will uncover biographies of writers and summaries of their writings.

Teacher Tip

Give students the task of an on-screen presentation of a poem by attaching visual and musical enhancements. They could use their own digital resources or material from YouTube. While YouTube can be a useful resource, make sure to supervise your students to ensure that they do not access any inappropriate content.

Audio recordings

There are several online sources of audio material where poets are recorded reading their own work. (Note: poets are not necessarily the best readers of their own work – most English teachers bring more expression to their reading than some great writers!) One good audio source is *The Poetry Archive*, and you can also try recorded material on *Poetry Speaks Expanded*, edited by Elise Paschen and Rebekah Mosby.

Audiobooks

In addition, most classic English Literature texts (novels and drama) are available in audiobook form. You can check out what's available on Google Play and iTunes.

Mobile applications

Smartphone apps to aid study are available at reasonable prices and, best of all, various versions of the complete works of William Shakespeare can be downloaded to a smartphone. These generally include a search facility and additional material, such as plot summaries and character notes.

Video recordings

Most classic English Literature texts are commercially available in DVD form. Clips from them are plentiful on the internet. It is particularly useful to play the same scene from two video recordings so that students can compare editing, interpretation and faithfulness to the text.

Blogs

You or your students may find some of the better literary blogs interesting. Here are some suggestions to get you started:

- Merryn Williams' list of the top 10 Literature blogs.
- Cornflower Books' list of the top 20 Literature blogs.
- Feedspot's Top 100 literary blogs.
- Electric Literature's Recommended Reading: 25 best websites for Literature lovers.
- Open Culture's 20+ Great Book & Literature Blogs: a list of idiosyncratic and specialist literary blogs.

The power of Word

If you have access to interactive whiteboards, these are excellent for displaying a text to the whole class. You can ask individual students to use the touchscreen to make changes to a text or add words to a 'cloze' version of a text. They also allow you to show adapted texts by clicking on any of the Microsoft Word functions described below. Regardless of whether you have this proprietary software, there are various ways in which word processing functions can be used to create lesson activities and to highlight features of literary texts.

Find > Replace

This allows you (or your students) to modify a text by altering one feature.

For example, take a passage from an online version of a novel and change it from past tense to present tense, or from first person to third person. Students can then compare the two and decide which one they prefer.

Teacher Tip

For example, if you are using Word, use 'Find' then 'Replace' to change 'I' to 'he' or 'she' in one of the prose passages from the lesson ideas. Remember to make other necessary changes (such as changing verb endings) to the passage. You could ask your students to compare the two passages and discuss their responses as a group.

11

Changing font colour

Using different font colours from the toolbar is a good way of drawing attention to language and stylistic features of a text. For example, you could present on paper or screen three versions of a text, one with verbs highlighted in red, one with adjectives in blue and one with similes and metaphors in green.

Another use of this feature is to select *white highlight* for words you want to remove. You can use this version as a 'cloze' procedure exercise where students guess the missing words. You can reveal them one at a time on screen by undoing the highlight and restoring the printed word.

Teacher Tip

Other functions useful for displaying features of digital texts are the 'Highlight' and 'Text Effects' buttons on the toolbar. These provide a way of displaying a text with emphasis on linguistic features (e.g. verbs, nouns, adjectives, adverbs, pronouns, prepositions) or structural content features (e.g. ideas, feelings and attitudes).

Teacher Tip

Text collapse and **Sort**

This is a very helpful way of drawing attention to the range and type of words exploited by a writer. It's also a simple and unthreatening way of engaging students with authorial choice and some creative writing arising from literary study.

To 'Collapse' a text into alphabetical order using Word:

Make sure it is a 'clean' text – i.e. not directly copied from the internet (see *Troubleshooting*).

Using the 'Edit' menu, select 'Find' and 'Replace'. Type a space in the 'Find what' box.

Type ^p in the 'Replace with' box (NB: a lower case p).

Click on 'Replace All'. This will put the text into a long thin column.

Using the 'Table' menu, select the 'Sort' function to sort the words alphabetically.

Go back to 'Find and Replace' and reverse what you did before: Type ^p in the 'Find what' box.

Type a space in the 'Replace with' box.

Click on 'Replace All'.

This will put the text into a paragraph-like block, which is easier to work with.

Save your new text with a new filename.

Troubleshooting

The most likely causes of the process not working are:

- A space was left in the 'Find what' box just next to the ^p. Spaces are small and invisible, so just check.
- You have inadvertently selected a part of the document somewhere and the program is applying your instructions just to that one bit. Make sure none of your text is selected, or that **all** of it is.

Source: Millum, T. and Warren, C. (2014) *Sharing not Staring: 21 Interactive Whiteboard Lessons for the English Classroom* 2nd edition. (London: Routledge)

Collapsing and reconstructing a text

Here is the first part of Moniza Alvi's poem, 'Presents from my aunts in Pakistan':

They sent me a salwar kameez
        peacock–blue,
                and another
    glistening like an orange split open,
embossed slippers, gold and black
        points curling.

> Candy-striped glass bangles
> > snapped, drew blood.
> Like at school, fashions changed

This is collapsed text, in alphabetical order:

> a an and and another at bangles black blood. Candy-striped changed curling. drew embossed fashions glass glistening gold kameez like Like me open, orange peacock-blue, points salwar school, sent slippers, snapped, split They

Students can now reconstruct the original text, testing their memory and understanding.

Alternatively, they can construct a text of their own using each of the words in the collapsed text once only. They should cross out words in the collapsed master when they have used them.

To tidy up your collapsed text, you could use 'Format' > 'Change case' to put it all in lower case and 'Find and Replace' to remove full stops, commas etc.

Teacher Tip

Students like using slide presentation software because it gives a professional-looking finish. Sometimes that gives an easy and flattering appearance to some otherwise weak content. Give students instruction that ensures a focus and structure relevant to their Literature study:

> You have ten slides to make up a presentation on your texts.
>
> Your ten slides must include slides dedicated to:
>
> - the writer's ideas/attitudes/feelings
> - genre, form and structure
> - the writer's craft
> - relevance to me
> - relevance to others.
>
> You can use the five remaining slides in any way you like but the whole presentation package must include ten references to the text.

Giving your students a pre-formatted slide package will allow them to do some focused and structured homework that does not add to your considerable marking burden.

Embedded texts

An **embedded text** is one where the words of a text for study are dropped into another invented text, that keeps all the original words but adds more text in between the parts of the original. It's a 'cut and paste' insertion of one text into another. You can embed a poem in an invented prose wrap so that students have to select and paste the original poem by using cues of rhyme and diction. This example is based on the poem, 'Nettles' by Vernon Scannell.

I was talking to my neighbour yesterday and he said he's had a bad experience. 'My son aged three fell in the nettle bed' he said. I thought to myself that 'Bed' seemed a curious name for those green spears, because it's a sort of comfortable word for that regiment of spite behind the shed. It suggests a place to rest, but a nettle-bed? Certainly, it was no place for rest that I would fancy. Anyway, my neighbour told me that with sobs and tears

The boy came seeking comfort. My neighbour pointed to his arms and legs as he remembered, 'and I saw

White blisters beaded on his tender skin.' His partner came out to see what was going on and we soothed him till his pain was not so raw. Gradually, the little boy stopped sobbing and crying, until they saw that he was feeling better, and 'At last he offered us a watery grin.' My neighbour then went on to say what he did next.

'And then I took my billhook,' he said, showing me the item, he honed the blade and went outside and slashed in fury with it. Well, he set about that nettle patch with a real sense of mission, as if getting his revenge on the nettles that had hurt his little boy. He slashed till not a nettle in that fierce parade stood upright any more.

'I bet that made you feel better,' I said. He was still reliving the memory. 'And then I lit a funeral pyre to burn the fallen dead.'

'So that was the end of the episode then,' I said, thinking he's got the business out of his system.

'Well, sort of,' he went on, 'But in two weeks the busy sun and rain had called up tall recruits behind the shed.'

'Ah, yes' I said. 'So the whole thing could happen again?'

'Well, probably not, because he's learned that nettles can hurt. But there are other things waiting in life to hurt him in other ways. I want to protect him, but I've got to accept that I can't always do that and my son would often feel sharp wounds again.'

These lesson ideas are suitable for classroom work, but are also suitable for homework if students take away digital copies. The advantage is that they prepare for a lesson that can be easily marked and assessed. English teachers, generally, need to reduce their marking load and make assessment simpler!

▣ LESSON IDEA ONLINE 11.1: TEXT VERSIONS COMPARED

This lesson idea focuses on ways in which William Wordsworth adapted his most famous poem, 'I Wandered Lonely as a Cloud'. Students can decide whether the later version is any better than the first version.

▣ LESSON IDEA ONLINE 11.2: UNDERSTANDING HOW NARRATIVE AND DIALOGUE WORK – PROSE

Use this lesson idea to help students understand how narrative and dialogue work.

▣ LESSON IDEA ONLINE 11.3: VOCABULARY RECOGNITION AND MEMORY – DRAMA

Use this lesson idea to help students' vocabulary recognition and memory.

Digital technology is a fast-growing part of education. A quick look at an app repository will show numerous applications helpful to literary study – lists of quotations, key words, plot summaries, and so on. They also allow classroom resources to be made, such as word searches, crossword puzzles and variant texts such as cartoons. This is an area in which students themselves may know more than their teachers, which is an aid to promoting independence and co-learning.

Talk to colleagues in your school's IT department and ask for your classroom to be equipped with three tools for supporting teaching and learning – a digital projector, an interactive smartboard and a visualiser. A visualiser, which is a camera connected to a projector, will cut down your take-home marking and help you to offer advice as soon as students have written something in class. Other opportunities for developing your digital technology skills may be available online, or in published or face-to-face training.

Summary

In this chapter you have looked at some of the key considerations for how digital technology can support teaching of English Literature. You have considered:

- examples of digital resources and digital procedures that can generate useful classroom stimulus materials

- suitable materials for homework activities that require less time for marking than continuous prose

- ways of engaging students with details of language and authorial craft.

12 | Global thinking

What is global thinking?

Global thinking is about learning how to live in a complex world as an active and engaged citizen. It is about considering the bigger picture and appreciating the nature and depth of our shared humanity.

When we encourage global thinking in students we help them recognise, examine and express their own and others' perspectives. We need to scaffold students' thinking to enable them to engage on cognitive, social and emotional levels, and construct their understanding of the world to be able to participate fully in its future.

We as teachers can help students develop routines and habits of mind to enable them to move beyond the familiar, discern that which is of local and global significance, make comparisons, take a cultural perspective and challenge stereotypes. We can encourage them to learn about contexts and traditions, and provide opportunities for them to reflect on their own and others' viewpoints.

Why adopt a global thinking approach?

Global thinking is particularly relevant in an interconnected, digitised world where ideas, opinions and trends are rapidly and relentlessly circulated. Students learn to pause and evaluate. They study why a topic is important on a personal, local and global scale, and they will be motivated to understand the world and their significance in it. Students gain a deeper understanding of why different viewpoints and ideas are held across the world.

Global thinking is something we can nurture both within and across disciplines. We can invite students to learn how to use different lenses from each discipline to see and interpret the world. They also learn how best to apply and communicate key concepts within and across disciplines. We can help our students select the appropriate media and technology to communicate and create their own personal synthesis of the information they have gathered.

Global thinking enables students to become more rounded individuals who perceive themselves as actors in a global context and who value diversity. It encourages them to become more aware, curious and interested in learning about the world and how it works. It helps students to challenge assumptions and stereotypes, to be better informed and more respectful. Global thinking takes the focus beyond exams and grades, or even checklists of skills and attributes. It develops students who are more ready to compete in the global marketplace and more able to participate effectively in an interconnected world.

What are the challenges of incorporating global thinking?

The pressures of an already full curriculum, the need to meet national and local standards, and the demands of exam preparation may make it seem challenging to find time to incorporate global thinking into lessons and programmes of study. A whole-school approach may be required for global thinking to be incorporated in subject plans for teaching and learning.

We need to give all students the opportunity to find their voice and participate actively and confidently, regardless of their background and world experiences, when exploring issues of global significance. We need to design suitable activities that are clear, ongoing and varying. Students need to be able to connect with materials, and extend and challenge their thinking. We also need to devise and use new forms of assessment that incorporate flexible and cooperative thinking.

Literature and the world around

Literature is important because it gives us an insight into people, places and experiences that are different from our own. It lets us make an imaginative leap into other lives. It lets us travel to other lands. Sometimes the interest of the travel is in the strangeness or uniqueness of the people or places we find in literature. We may end up preferring the world we do live in, or wishing we lived in the world we visit through literature. Either way, our understanding has been widened.

Literature is also important because it allows us to compare our own lives with those we find in novels, poems and plays. By comparing, we may find that something written in one place, and at one time, may still be relevant to us in other places and at other times. It may be that we discover that the differences between people and places are less important than the similarities.

Think back to the way Literature is represented in the four-part model in Chapter 4 **Key considerations**. Obviously, the **global thinking** focus is most related to 'The World Around', but the links with that aspect include links to how the writer relates to the world around him or her, how the reader relates to the world around him or her, and how the text relates to the world around in publication, reputation and translation.

Teacher Tip

Ask students to find a text set in a particular culture. Ask them to explain aspects of the culture, and if they think the text has relevance beyond that culture.

Try the opening of a short story such as *Father's Help* by R.K. Narayan, *The Gold-Legged Frog* by Khamsingh Srinawak or *The Red Ball* by Ismith Khan.

Universal relevance

Wealth and technology, language and customs, faiths and cultures vary according to time and place. However, some things don't vary much across borders and oceans. Human needs, feelings and satisfactions do not change very much, wherever you find them. We all tend to prefer comfort to discomfort, and happiness to misery. Most of us hope in life to find love, success and security. Most of us would also admit to occasional feelings of envy, jealousy, resentment, impatience and disappointment. If you assume that these things are true of most human beings throughout history and across the globe, literature that deals with any of these aspects of humanity will have a universal relevance.

Teacher Tip

Jane Austen's novel *Pride and Prejudice* is set in England in the nineteenth century, a society where women did not work and could not inherit property. Where might students find similar relationships today?

Extended empathy

So, it helps to see that human beings and their societies may have all sorts of differences, but all sorts of things in common, too. Being able to see what is different and what is similar in other people is an important quality that depends on and develops empathy. When our feelings are engaged by people and events in fiction, we rehearse responses to similar people and events we may encounter in life. Understanding others and empathising with them, however different they are, is an important part of being a mature member of the human race and a citizen of the world.

Part of empathising with others is an understanding that they may respond to a text differently from how we might respond. Their interpretation may be affected by personal circumstance or by culture. Your students' response to reading will be improved if they can imagine and express responses and interpretations in addition to their own.

Reading a text and imagining how it may impact on different people can focus on:

- differences in cultures within the text
- similarities in cultures within the text
- different interpretations of texts coming from different cultures in the readers
- aspects of human behaviour and response that give texts global relevance.

Teacher Tip

Ask students to translate 'To be, or not to be ...' into as many languages as they can think of. Put the results on a sheet of A3 paper with an arrow pointing to a map of the world to show where the quotation now fits. (Don't forget Stratford-upon-Avon in England.) Then add to the A3 sheet arrows indicating countries where *Hamlet* has been translated into the local language (there will be a lot of arrows!). For example:

Sein oder nicht sein ...
Être ou ne pas être ...
Ser o no ser ...
Essere o non essere ...
... يكون أو لا يكون

Understanding and empathising with others are helped by being able to explore different **contexts** and the way that texts may or may not have a relevance to them. Empathy and context are key ideas in literary study, and shape understanding in ways that fit the assessment objectives. Showing this in their written response is a strong feature of students' writing about reading. Here are some examples of writing about John Steinbeck's novel, *Of Mice and Men*.

From understanding to empathising

George gets annoyed with Lennie sometimes because he gets on his nerves. Sometimes he wishes he didn't have to look after him.

Sometimes George gets frustrated with Lennie's slowness ("for God's sake!") and sometimes he is patient ("don't drink too much") and sometimes he protects him against other people. This doesn't mean he is impatient but that he always cares, even if it's a strain on him. It shows he feels he has a duty to look after Lennie, however hard it gets and however frustrating he finds it. I think I would find it frustrating too.

From understanding to contextualising

In the novella Steinbeck shows that people can be lonely. He shows that they need dreams to cope with a hard life. He shows that most people get dragged down by their friends or companions.

It would be wrong to think that Steinbeck shows a pessimistic side to life by describing people who are lonely, and fantasists, and lumbered with useless relationships. He does this to create a sense of pity for society's underdogs, and a sense of admiration for the way people cling to their dreams however they are proved to be unrealistic. Some writers celebrate success, and winners. Steinbeck wants to create sympathy with those who share the American Dream but are not going to be winners. He's challenging the view that everyone can make it in the great democracy of America and pointing out that there are casualties and victims who may have as much to tell us about the human spirit as those who make it to the White House.

Teacher Tip

Read the story of *Little Red Riding Hood*, taking a version from the internet. Ask students to set the plot and characters in a regional/cultural setting of their choice. You could try Paris, Brussels, Singapore, Dubai or Kuala Lumpur. Little Red Riding Hood could be a typical teenage girl living in any of those places, and the Wolf could be a local form of villain.

Responding with empathy

The best responses show that students are personally engaged with ideas, attitudes and feelings – both those in the texts and in the mind of the writer. The ability to empathise with others – even with others with whom you disagree – is a strong sign of a more personal and developed response.

Students may be able to comment on empathy with characters and situations in films or other screen fiction/digital resources they know. It would be good to link this empathy with fictional characters to empathy with real people and situations, such as migrants, disaster victims or people living in harsh conditions. What is important is that students realise that empathy can be triggered by real or fictional events, and that empathetic responses are as important as intellectual responses if we are to be caring global citizens.

Teacher Tip

Ask students to find texts from three different cultures that portray the causes and effects of a powerful emotion such as fear, loyalty, revenge, pride or ambition. For example, *Anil* by Ridjal Noor or *Invisible Mass of the Back Row* by Claudette Williams.

☑ LESSON IDEA ONLINE 12.1: THE 'WORLD WITHIN' AND THE 'WORLD AROUND' IN PROSE FICTION

Father's Help, by R. K. Narayan, has several features that make it specific to a locality and a time. This lesson idea supports students to see that prose fiction may have distinctive features of setting, character and language which extend our understanding and empathy. The text also deals with attitudes and feelings about family relationships, children's thoughts and feelings, and ways in which a lie can turn out to have alarming consequences.

☑ LESSON IDEA ONLINE 12.2: THE 'WORLD WITHIN' AND THE 'WORLD AROUND' IN POETRY

'Night of the Scorpion', by Nissim Ezekiel, also has several features that make it specific to a locality and a time. This lesson idea explores features of setting, character and language in poetry, which extend our understanding and empathy. The text also deals with attitudes and feelings about family relationships, children's thoughts and feelings, and ways in which an event made the writer see his parents and his community in a different light.

⚏ **LESSON IDEA ONLINE 12.3: THE 'WORLD WITHIN' AND THE 'WORLD AROUND' IN DRAMA**

This lesson idea supports students to overcome negative responses to unfamiliar names and places in Shakespeare plays, by showing how ideas, attitudes and feelings are similar to those within students' own lives.

Local and global thinking in English Literature

Students in international schools probably have a stronger sense of global thinking than those in other schools. They are likely to be familiar with cultural and linguistic diversity, and may be familiar with other literatures than those they study in their English Literature syllabus. This gives them an advantage when studying set texts in English Literature because they will be able to see how much of the text seems very specifically UK-focused and relevant, and how much goes beyond the limits of geography and culture. For example, Shakespeare uses an unfamiliar language and creates characters with names like Romeo, Macbeth and Hamlet that are unfamiliar outside of Italy, Scotland or Denmark, but their feelings and motives may be much more familiar – love, ambition and revenge are truly global human features!

This ability to see what is culturally local and what is thematically global will help students judge the merits of works of literature from the past. This requires a similar ability to identify features exclusive to the historical setting and features inclusive of global experience and understanding.

These two dimensions of study go to the centre of what literature does and why it matters. Literature connects readers everywhere with the experiences, thoughts and feelings of others across time and space. Some of these may be similar and some different, but all are important in belonging to a global community.

Summary

This chapter has demonstrated that, although differences in people, settings and language can make texts seem strange to students, core ideas, attitudes and feelings are universal and can be relevant to their own lives. Remember that:

- there are differences and similarities in cultures within literary texts

- empathy and context are key ideas in Literature study

- the best responses to reading a text show that students are personally engaged with its ideas, attitudes and feelings.

13 | Reflective practice

Dr Paul Beedle, Head of Professional Development Qualifications, Cambridge International

'As a teacher you are always learning'

It is easy to say this, isn't it? Is it true? Are you bound to learn just by being a teacher?

You can learn every day from the experience of working with your students, collaborating with your colleagues and playing your part in the life of your school. You can learn also by being receptive to new ideas and approaches, and by applying and evaluating these in practice in your own context.

To be more precise, let us say that as a teacher:

- you **should** always be learning
  to develop your expertise throughout your career for your own fulfilment as a member of the teaching profession and to be as effective as possible in the classroom.
- you **can** always be learning
  if you approach the teaching experience with an open mind, ready to learn and knowing how to reflect on what you are doing in order to improve.

You want your professional development activities to be as relevant as possible to what you do and who you are, and to help change the quality of your teaching and your students' learning – for the better, in terms of outcomes, and for good, in terms of lasting effect. You want to feel that 'it all makes sense' and that you are actively following a path that works for you personally, professionally and career-wise.

So professional learning is about making the most of opportunities and your working environment, bearing in mind who you are, what you are like and how you want to improve. But simply experiencing – thinking about and responding to situations, and absorbing ideas and information – is not necessarily learning. It is through reflection that you can make the most of your experience to deepen and extend your professional skills and understanding.

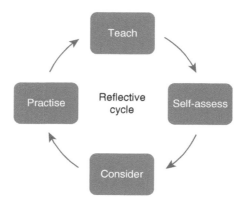

Figure 13.1

In this chapter, we will focus on three *essentials* of reflective practice, explaining in principle and in practice how you can support your own continuing professional development:

1 **Focusing** on what you want to learn about and why.
2 **Challenging** yourself and others to go beyond description and assumptions to critical analysis and evaluation.
3 **Sharing** what you are learning with colleagues – to enrich understanding and enhance the quality of practice.

These essentials will help you as you apply and adapt the rich ideas and approaches in this book in your own particular context. They will also help you if you are, or are about to be, taking part in a Cambridge Professional Development Qualification (Cambridge PDQ) programme, to make the most of your programme, develop your portfolio and gain the qualification.

1 Focus
In principle

Given the multiple dimensions and demands of being a teacher, you might be tempted to try to cover 'everything' in your professional development but you will then not have the time to go beneath the surface much at all. Likewise, attending many different training events will certainly keep you very busy but it is unlikely that these will simply add up to improving your thinking and practice in sustainable and systematic ways.

Teachers who are beginning an organised programme of professional learning find that it is most helpful to select particular ideas, approaches and topics which are relevant to their own situation and their school's priorities. They can then be clear about their professional learning goals, and how their own learning contributes to improving their students' learning outcomes. They deliberately choose activities that help make sense of their practice with their students in their school and have a clear overall purpose.

It is one thing achieving focus, and another maintaining this over time. When the going gets tough, because it is difficult either to understand or become familiar with new ideas and practices, or to balance learning time with the demands of work and life, it really helps to have a mission – to know why you want to learn something as well as what that something is. Make sure that this is a purpose which you feel genuinely belongs to you and in which you have a keen interest, rather than it being something given to you or imposed on you. Articulate your focus not just by writing it down but by 'pitching' it to a colleague whose opinion you trust and taking note of their feedback.

In practice

- Plan
  What is my goal and how will I approach the activity?

  Select an approach that is new to you, but make sure that you understand the thinking behind this and that it is relevant to your students' learning. Do it for real effect, not for show.

- Monitor
  Am I making progress towards my goal; do I need to try a different approach?

  Take time during your professional development programme to review how far and well you are developing your understanding of theory and practice. What can you do to get more out of the experience, for example by discussing issues with your mentor, researching particular points, and asking your colleagues for their advice?

- Evaluate
  What went well, what could have been better, what have I learned for next time?

  Evaluation can sometimes be seen as a 'duty to perform' – like clearing up after the event – rather than the pivotal moment in learning that it really is. Evaluate not because you are told you have to; evaluate to make sense of the learning experience you have been through and what it means to you, and to plan ahead to see what you can do in the future.

Approaches to learning and teaching Literature in English

This cycle of planning, monitoring and evaluation is just as relevant to you as a professional learner as to your students as learners. Be actively in charge of your learning and take appropriate actions. Make your professional development work for you. Of course your professional development programme leaders, trainers and mentors will guide and support you in your learning, but you are at the heart of your own learning experience, not on the receiving end of something that is cast in stone. Those who assist and advise you on your professional development want you and your colleagues to get the best out of the experience, and need your feedback along the way so that if necessary they can adapt and improve what they are devising.

2 Challenge
In principle

Reflection is a constructive process that helps the individual teacher to improve their thinking and practice. It involves regularly asking questions of yourself about your developing ideas and experience, and keeping track of your developing thinking, for example in a reflective journal. Reflection is continuous, rather than a one-off experience. Being honest with yourself means thinking hard, prompting yourself to go beyond your first thoughts about a new experience and to avoid taking for granted your opinions about something to which you are accustomed. Be a critical friend to yourself.

In the Cambridge PDQ Certificate in Teaching and Learning, for example, teachers take a fresh look at the concepts and processes of learning and challenge their own assumptions. They engage with theory and models of effective teaching and learning, and open their minds through observing experienced practitioners, applying new ideas in practice and listening to formative feedback from mentors and colleagues. To evidence in their assessed portfolio how they have learned from this experience, they not only present records of observed practice but also critical analysis showing understanding of how and why practices work and how they can be put into different contexts successfully.

The Cambridge PDQ syllabuses set out key questions to focus professional learning and the portfolio templates prompts to help you. These questions provide a framework for reflection. They are open-ended and will not only stimulate your thinking but lead to lively group discussion. The discipline of asking yourself and others questions such as 'Why?' 'How do we know?' 'What is the evidence?' 'What are the conditions?' leads to thoughtful and intelligent practice.

In practice
Challenge:

- Yourself, as you reflect on an experience, to be more critical in your thinking. For example, rather than simply describing what happened, analyse why it happened and its significance, and what might have happened if conditions had been different.
- Theory – by understanding and analysing the argument, and evaluating the evidence that supports the theory. Don't simply accept a theory as a given fact – be sure that you feel that the ideas make sense and that there is positive value in applying them in practice.
- Convention – the concept of 'best practice(s)' is as good as we know now, on the basis of the body of evidence, for example on the effect size of impact of a particular approach on learning outcomes (defined in the next chapter). By using an approach in an informed way and with a critical eye, you can evaluate the approach relating to your particular situation.

3   Share
In principle

Schools are such busy places, and yet teachers can feel they are working on their own for long periods because of the intensity of their workload as they focus on all that is involved in teaching their students. We know that a crucial part of our students' active learning is the opportunity to collaborate with their peers in order to investigate, create and communicate. Just so with professional learning: teachers learn best through engagement with their peers, in their own school and beyond. Discussion and interaction with colleagues, focused on learning and student outcomes, and carried out in a culture of openness, trust and respect, helps each member of the community of practice in the school clarify and sharpen their understanding and enhance their practice.

This is why the best professional learning programmes incorporate collaborative learning, and pivotal moments are designed into the programme for this to happen frequently over time: formally in guided learning sessions such as workshops and more informally in opportunities such as study group, teach meets and discussion, both face-to-face and online.

In practice

Go beyond expectations!

In the Cambridge PDQ syllabus, each candidate needs to carry out an observation of an experienced practitioner and to be observed formatively themselves by their mentor on a small number of occasions. This is the formal requirement in terms of evidence of practice within the portfolio for the qualification. The expectation is that these are not the only times that teachers will observe and be observed for professional learning purposes (rather than performance appraisal).

However, the more that teachers can observe each other's teaching, the better; sharing of practice leads to advancement of shared knowledge and understanding of aspects of teaching and learning, and development of agreed shared 'best practice'.

So:

- open your classroom door to observation
- share with your closest colleague(s) when you are trying out a fresh approach, such as an idea in this book
- ask them to look for particular aspects in the lesson, especially how students are engaging with the approach – pose an observation question
- reflect with them after the lesson on what you and they have learned from the experience – pose an evaluation question
- go and observe them as they do the same
- after a number of lessons, discuss with your colleagues how you can build on your peer observation with common purpose (for example, lesson study).
- share with your other colleagues in the school what you are gaining from this collaboration and encourage them to do the same
- always have question(s) to focus observations and focus these question(s) on student outcomes.

Pathways

The short-term effects of professional development are very much centred on teachers' students. For example, the professional learning in a Cambridge PDQ programme should lead directly and quickly to changes in the ways your students learn. All teachers have this at heart – the desire to help their students learn better.

The long-term effects of professional development are more teacher-centric. During their career over, say, 30 years, a teacher may teach many thousand lessons. There are many good reasons for a teacher to keep up-to-date with pedagogy, not least to sustain their enjoyment of what they do.

Each teacher will follow their own career pathway, taking into account many factors. We do work within systems, at school and wider level, involving salary and appointment levels, and professional development can be linked to these as requirement or expectation. However, to a significant extent teachers shape their own career pathway, making decisions along the way. Their pathway is not pre-ordained; there is room for personal choice, opportunity and serendipity. It is for each teacher to judge for themselves how much they wish to venture. A teacher's professional development pathway should reflect and support this.

It is a big decision to embark on an extended programme of professional development, involving a significant commitment of hours of learning and preparation over several months. You need to be as clear as you can be about the immediate and long-term value of such a commitment. Will your programme lead to academic credit as part of a stepped pathway towards Masters level, for example?

Throughout your career, you need to be mindful of the opportunities you have for professional development. Gauge the value of options available at each particular stage in your professional life, both in terms of relevance to your current situation – your students, subject and phase focus, and school – and the future situation(s) of which you are thinking.

14 Understanding the impact of classroom practice on student progress

Lee Davis, Deputy Director for Education, Cambridge International

Introduction

Throughout this book, you have been encouraged to adopt a more active approach to teaching and learning and to ensure that formative assessment is embedded into your classroom practice. In addition, you have been asked to develop your students as meta-learners, such that they are able to, as the academic Chris Watkins puts it, 'narrate their own learning' and become more reflective and strategic in how they plan, carry out and then review any given learning activity.

A key question remains, however. How will you know that the new strategies and approaches you intend to adopt have made a significant difference to your students' progress and learning? What, in other words, has been the impact and how will you know?

This chapter looks at how you might go about determining this at the classroom level. It deliberately avoids reference to whole-school student tracking systems, because these are not readily available to all schools and all teachers. Instead, it considers what you can do as an individual teacher to make the learning of your students visible – both to you and anyone else who is interested in how they are doing. It does so by introducing the concept of 'effect sizes' and shows how these can be used by teachers to determine not just whether an intervention works or not but, more importantly, *how well* it works. 'Effect size' is a useful way of quantifying or measuring the size of any difference between two groups or data sets. The aim is to place emphasis on the most important aspect of an intervention or change in teaching approach – the **size of the effect** on student outcomes.

Consider the following scenario:

Over the course of a term, a teacher has worked hard with her students on understanding 'what success looks like' for any given task or activity. She has stressed the importance of everyone being clear about the criteria for success, before students embark upon the chosen task and plan their way through it. She has even got to the point where students have been co-authors of the assessment rubrics used, so that they have been fully engaged in the intended outcomes throughout and can articulate what is required before they have even started. The teacher is happy with developments so far, but has it made a difference to student progress? Has learning increased beyond what we would normally expect for an average student over a term anyway?

Here is an extract from the teacher's markbook.

Student	Sept Task	Nov Task
Katya	13	15
Maria	15	20
Joao	17	23
David	20	18
Mushtaq	23	25
Caio	25	38
Cristina	28	42
Tom	30	35
Hema	32	37
Jennifer	35	40

Figure 14.1

Before we start analysing this data, we must note the following:

- The task given in September was at the start of the term – the task in November was towards the end of the term.
- Both tasks assessed similar skills, knowledge and understanding in the student.
- The maximum mark for each was 50.
- The only variable that has changed over the course of the term is the approaches to teaching and learning by the teacher. All other things are equal.

With that in mind, looking at Figure 14.1, what conclusions might you draw as an external observer?

You might be saying something along the lines of: 'Mushtaq and Katya have made some progress, but not very much. Caio and Cristina appear to have done particularly well. David, on the other hand, appears to be going backwards!'

What can you say about the class as a whole?

Calculating effect sizes

What if we were to apply the concept of 'effect sizes' to the class results in Figure 13.1, so that we could make some more definitive statements about the impact of the interventions over the given time period? Remember, we are doing so in order to understand the size of the effect on student outcomes or progress.

Let's start by understanding how it is calculated.

An effect size is found by calculating 'the standardised mean difference between two data sets or groups'. In essence, this means we are looking for the difference between two averages, while taking into the account the spread of values (in this case, marks) around those averages at the same time.

As a formula, and from Figure 14.1, it looks like the following:

$$\text{Effect size} = \frac{\text{average class mark (after intervention)} - \text{average class mark (before intervention)}}{\text{spread (standard deviation of the class)}}$$

In words: the average mark achieved by the class *before* the teacher introduced her intervention strategies is taken away from the average mark achieved by the class *after* the intervention strategies. This is then divided by the standard deviation[1] of the class as a whole.

---

[1] The standard deviation is merely a way of expressing by how much the members of a group (in this case, student marks in the class) differ from the average value (or mark) for the group.

Inserting our data into a spreadsheet helps us calculate the effect size as follows:

	A	B	C
1	Student	September Task	November Task
2	Katya	13	15
3	Maria	15	20
4	Joao	17	23
5	David	20	18
6	Mushtaq	23	25
7	Caio	25	38
8	Cristina	28	42
9	Tom	30	35
10	Hema	32	37
11	Jennifer	35	40
12			
13	Average mark	23.8 = AVERAGE (B2:B11)	29.3 = AVERAGE (C2:C11)
14	Standard deviation	7.5 = STDEV (B2:B11)	10.11 = STDEV (C2:C11)

Figure 14.2

Therefore, the effect size for this class $= \dfrac{29.3 - 23.8}{8.8} = 0.62$
But what does this mean?

Interpreting effect sizes for classroom practice

In pure statistical terms, a 0.62 effect size means that the average student mark **after** the intervention by the teacher, is 0.62 standard deviations above the average student mark **before** the intervention.

We can state this in another way: the post-intervention average mark now exceeds 61% of the student marks previously.

Going further, we can also say that the average student mark, post-intervention, would have placed a student in the top four in the class previously. You can see this visually in Figure 14.2 where 29.3 (the class average after the teacher's interventions) would have been between Cristina's and Tom's marks in the September task.

This is good, isn't it? As a teacher, would you be happy with this progress by the class over the term?

To help understand effect sizes further, and therefore how well or otherwise the teacher has done above, let us look at how they are used in large-scale studies as well as research into educational effectiveness more broadly. We will then turn our attention to what really matters – talking about student learning.

Effect sizes in research

We know from results analyses of the Program for International Student Assessment (PISA) and the Trends in International Mathematics and Science Study (TIMMS) that, across the world, a year's schooling leads to an effect size of 0.4. John Hattie and his team at The University of Melbourne reached similar conclusions when looking at over 900 meta-analyses of classroom and whole-school interventions to improve student learning – 240 million students later, the result was an effect size of 0.4 on average for all these strategies.

What this means, then, is that any teacher achieving an effect size of greater than 0.4 is doing better than expected (than the average) over the course of a year. From our earlier example, not only are the students making better than expected progress, they are also doing so in just one term.

Here is something else to consider. In England, the distribution of GCSE grades in Maths and English have standard deviations of between 1.5 and 1.8 grades (A*, A, B, C, etc.), so an improvement of one GCSE grade represents an effect size of between 0.5 and 0.7. This means that, in the context of secondary schools, introducing a change in classroom practice of 0.62 (as the teacher achieved above) would result in an improvement of about one GCSE grade for each student in the subject.

Furthermore, for a school in which 50% of students were previously attaining five or more A*–C grades, this percentage (assuming the effect size of 0.62 applied equally across all subjects and all other things being equal) would rise to 73%.

Now, that's something worth knowing.

What next for your classroom practice? Talking about student learning

Given what we now know about 'effect sizes', what might be the practical next steps for you as a teacher?

Firstly, try calculating 'effect sizes' for yourself, using marks and scores for your students that are comparable, e.g. student performance on key skills in Maths, Reading, Writing, Science practicals, etc. Become familiar with how they are calculated so that you can then start interrogating them 'intelligently'.

Do the results indicate progress was made? If so, how much is attributable to the interventions you have introduced?

Try calculating 'effect sizes' for each individual student, in addition to your class, to make their progress visible too. To help illustrate this, let us return to the comments we were making about the progress of some students in Figure 14.1. We thought Cristina and Caio did very well and we had grave concerns about David. Individual effect sizes for the class of students would help us shed light on this further:

Student	September Task	November task	Individual Effect Size
Katya	13	15	0.22*
Maria	15	20	0.55
Joao	17	23	0.66
David	20	18	-0.22
Mushtaq	23	25	0.22
Caio	25	38	1.43
Cristina	28	42	1.54
Tom	30	35	0.55
Hema	32	37	0.55
Jennifer	35	40	0.55

* The individual 'effect size' for each student above is calculated by taking their September mark away from their November mark and then dividing by the standard deviation for the class – in this case, 8.8.

Figure 14.3

If these were your students, what questions would you now ask of yourself, of your students and even of your colleagues, to help you understand why the results are as they are and how learning is best achieved? Remember, an effect size of 0.4 is our benchmark, so who is doing better than that? Who is not making the progress we would expect?

David's situation immediately stands out, doesn't it? A negative effect size implies learning has regressed. So, what has happened, and how will we draw alongside him to find out what the issues are and how best to address them?

Why did Caio and Cristina do so well, considering they were just above average previously? Effect sizes of 1.43 and 1.54 respectively are significantly above the benchmark, so what has changed from their perspective? Perhaps they responded particularly positively to developing assessment rubrics together. Perhaps learning had sometimes been a mystery to them before, but with success criteria now made clear, this obstacle to learning had been removed.

We don't know the answers to these questions, but they would be great to ask, wouldn't they? So go ahead and ask them. Engage in dialogue with your students, and see how their own ability to discuss their learning has changed and developed. This will be as powerful a way as any of discovering whether your new approaches to teaching and learning have had an impact and it ultimately puts data, such as 'effect sizes', into context.

Concluding remarks

'Effect sizes' are a very effective means of helping you understand the impact of your classroom practice upon student progress. If you change your teaching strategies in some way, calculating 'effect sizes', for both the class and each individual student, helps you determine not just *if* learning has improved, but by *how much*.

They are, though, only part of the process. As teachers, we must look at the data carefully and intelligently in order to understand 'why'. Why did some students do better than others? Why did some not make any progress at all? Use 'effect sizes' as a starting point, not the end in itself.

Ensure that you don't do this in isolation – collaborate with others and share this approach with them. What are your colleagues finding in their classes, in their subjects? Are the same students making the same progress across the curriculum? If there are differences, what might account for them?

In answering such questions, we will be in a much better position to determine next steps in the learning process for students. After all, isn't that our primary purpose as teachers?

Acknowledgements, further reading and resources

This chapter has drawn extensively on the influential work of the academics John Hattie and Robert Coe. You are encouraged to look at the following resources to develop your understanding further:

Hattie, J. (2012) *Visible Learning for Teachers – Maximising Impact on Learning*. London and New York: Routledge.

Coe, R. (2002) *It's the Effect Size, Stupid. What effect size is and why it is important.* Paper presented at the Annual Conference of The British Educational Research Association, University of Exeter, England, 12–14 September, 2002. A version of the paper is available online on the University of Leeds website.

The Centre for Evaluation and Monitoring, University of Durham, has produced a very useful 'effect size' calculator (available from their website). Note that it also calculates a confidence interval for any 'effect size' generated. Confidence intervals are useful in helping you understand the margin for error of an 'effect size' you are reporting for your class. These are particularly important when the sample size is small, which will inevitably be the case for most classroom teachers.

15 | Recommended reading

For a deeper understanding of the Cambridge approach, refer to the Cambridge International website (http://www. cambridgeinternational.org/teaching-and-learning) where you will find the following resources:

Implementing the curriculum with Cambridge: a guide for school leaders.

Developing your school with Cambridge: a guide for school leaders.

Education Briefs for a number of topics, such as active learning and bilingual education. Each brief includes information about the challenges and benefits of different approaches to teaching, practical tips, lists of resources.

Getting started with … These are interactive resources to help explore and develop areas of teaching and learning. They include practical examples, reflective questions, and experiences from teachers and researchers.

For further support around becoming a Cambridge school, visit cambridge-community.org.uk.

The resources in this section can be used as a supplement to your learning, to build upon your awareness of Literature in English teaching and the pedagogical themes in this series.

Thomas, P. (2010). *The Complete Shakespearience: Active Approaches for the Classroom.* London: National Association for the Teaching of English (NATE).

Blake, J. (2006). *The Full English: An A to Z Handbook of English Teaching Activities.* London: National Association for the Teaching of English (NATE).

Millum, T. and Warren, C. (2012). *Unlocking Poetry: An Inspirational Resource for Teaching GCSE Literature.* London: Routledge.

Millum, T. and Warren, C. (2014). *Sharing not Staring: 21 Interactive Whiteboard Lessons for the English Classroom.* London: Routledge.

Teaching English magazine. London: National Association for the Teaching of English (NATE) (for members).

Watkins, C. (2015) *Meta-Learning in Classrooms.* The SAGE Handbook of Learning. Edited by Scott D. and Hargreaves E. London: Sage Publications.

Index